This is a truly important book and a must-read for anyone who cares about justice for the poor and vulnerable. Matt takes us into the darkest of places, shining an unforgiving light on a horrendous tragedy, involving girls as young as ten trapped in a cruel adult world. Prepare to be heartbroken by their stories, angered and appalled at the evil being done to them. Like me, you will be gutted to read of the suffering of these most vulnerable of victims, but you will also be heartened and inspired by Matt and his team's creative attempts to bring them hope. Over the next few years Brazil is going to be a focus of the world's attention. The scandal of child prostitution on the country's longest motorway can no longer go unspoken. This book should be the start of an international effort to bring it to an end.

Steve Chalke, *UN Special Advisor on Community Action Against Human Trafficking*

Compelling and poignant reportage that painstakingly exposes Brazil's darkest secret. Matt Roper is that rare journalist who didn't turn his back on the trauma and misery he witnessed for the adrenaline rush of the next deadline. In parts heart-breaking, in others uplifting, this is a story that needs to be told.

Oliver Harvey, *The Sun*

Few journalists remain this committed to exposing an issue. Once you get your headlines it is all too easy to move on to the next big expose. Not only is this a dark side of Brazil that Matt continues to highlight with passion, but his writi̶̶̶̶̶̶̶̶̶̶̶ ̶idly into children's lives. You are u̶ them. Few books can do th̶

D1432841

Chris Rogers, *BBC Panorama, n̶*

By the same author
*Street Girls*
*Remember Me, Rescue Me*

# HIGHWAY TO HELL

The road where childhoods are stolen

## MATT ROPER

MONARCH
B O O K S
Oxford, UK & Grand Rapids, Michigan, USA

Published by Monarch Books
an imprint of
**Lion Hudson plc**
Wilkinson House, Jordan Hill Road,
Oxford OX2 8DR, England
Email: monarch@lionhudson.com
www.lionhudson.com/monarch

ISBN 978 0 85721 254 2
e-ISBN 978 0 85721 514 7

First edition 2013

A catalogue record for this book is available from the British Library

Printed and bound in the UK, August 2013, LH26

# Contents

# Foreword

I have a daughter of my own; I think that's why I was so moved by Matt's previous book – *Remember Me, Rescue Me*. The nightmarish accounts I was reading of girls exploited at the most vulnerable of ages drew both anger and sadness from me. But I had only read a book. When I actually met the girls – it rocked my life to the core. Suddenly, the stage and the hectic world of recording and touring and stardom became background noise to the plight of these girls.

In the pages of *Highway to Hell*, Matt describes a journey that ultimately leads to hope and healing and restoration – a conclusion that is full of promise. But before that are the pages that are difficult to read – the accounts of injustice, heartbreak, scandal, brutality, and the very living nightmare of child prostitution in Brazil.

It may be hard to read sometimes but if you enter the world of these precious kids, you might discover the most amazing thrill of life – that there is an awakening from that world, and we can be a part of helping them find their way out.

Dean Brody

# Prologue

This book started as a journalistic work, a way of documenting a situation which I felt needed to be told. Canadian country singer Dean Brody and I planned to travel up the BR-116, a motorway which we had discovered had an alarming incidence of child prostitution. We would tell the girls' stories, expose some of the perpetrators, hopefully bring the problem out of the shadows.

But it quickly turned personal as the true depth and scale of this tragedy began to impact us in ways we had never expected. Within days we were both experiencing a sense of despair and brokenness deeper than anything we had ever had to deal with. Our lives changed forever as we came face to face with precious, beautiful young lives being torn apart before our eyes. And the book became the story of another journey, of an attempt to rescue them, and of the stirrings of hope amid the darkness.

Now much more than ever, I believe the world needs to hear about the BR-116. I truly hope and pray that what you are about to read will affect you just as deeply and irreversibly. For, in the words of Martin Luther King Jr, "the greatest tragedy" is "not the strident clamor of the bad people, but the appalling silence of the good people."

Matt Roper

**BR-116 motorway**

## Chapter 1

# The Girl in the Lilac Dress

S he came into our lives in the blink of an eye, a brief moment in time which suddenly, unexpectedly, pierced the pitch-black gloom. For one split second she was illuminated in our headlights, the next once again swallowed by the shadows.

We'd been driving for hours, straining through the darkness just to make out the faded white lines and rusting green road signs ahead of us. The BR-116 motorway twisted and dipped through dense forest and wide-open plains, although both were equally black in the dead of night. Occasionally we'd be blinded by a monster truck that roared past, spewing thick black fumes, or hurtled up behind us, braying and snorting like a stampeding bull. Most of the time I was leaning forward in my seat, gripping the wheel with both hands.

The dashboard clock flashed 01.23 as we went over the crest of a hill and the lights of a town – and our hotel for the night – shimmered invitingly in the distance. The mere thought of a bed instantly brought on the weariness that our bodies had managed to hold off until then.

And it was then that we saw her: a tiny young thing, standing motionless at the side of the road in front of us.

She was wearing a pretty lilac sundress which hung loosely on her small bones. It fluttered in the breeze as she began to wander towards the traffic, balancing herself on a raised concrete verge between the motorway and the clumps of tall grass which rose twice as high as her.

She looked no older than eleven.

As we drove past her face flashed towards us, a look of innocence, her jet-black hair neatly tied back and carefully parted on one side, a big purple ribbon in the other. She looked so out of place there – a child, dressed as if her mother had fussed over her – just inches away from that roaring river of traffic. Then, as quickly as she'd appeared in front of us, she was just a shadowy figure in my rear-view mirror.

Dean was the first to say something. "Did you see her? What was she doing there? Do you think she was…?"

"Prostituting? Oh, no, I don't think… I'm sure she's not," I said, my eyes still fixed above me as the little girl shrank away into the distance.

Dean sat back in his seat, apparently satisfied by my response. After all, I was his guide for this journey, the one who had travelled this route before, who knew Brazil, its people and its problems better than he did. He gazed out at the lights which were beginning to fill the blackness on both sides – yellow street lamps, illuminated shop signs, billboards. And I watched as the girl in the lilac dress finally disappeared into the distance.

The subject of child prostitution was what had brought us to this obscure Brazilian town in the first place. Governador Valadares was one of the many places I had visited during a journey around Brazil ten years before, researching the issue for what would eventually be published in a book. What I'd found had shocked me, particularly in Brazil's biggest cities like Rio and Recife, where young girls openly offered themselves to foreign tourists. Back then I'd visited Valadares because, although remote, it too received plenty of tourists – competitors in and spectators of international hang-gliding championships regularly packed the town's hotels, restaurants, and bars. And I'd left in no doubt that, like those other major tourist centres where outsiders arrived with money to spend, child prostitution was also a problem here.

But there was another aggravating factor – a major motorway which pulsed through the town's heart, bringing development and growth but also exploitation. Thousands of trucks would rumble through Governador Valadares along the BR-116 every day, bringing many more men than the chartered tourist flights that touched down at its airport. I'd met some of the girls, many from problem-afflicted families in the impoverished slums, who would stand beside the motorway, offering themselves for a few reals to the drivers passing through on long, lonely journeys.

None, though, were like the girl we'd just seen by the side of the road. They were young but hardened by life – tough, rebellious, cynical, scarred by their suffering. They didn't wear pretty ribbons in neatly combed hair. And besides, it's quite common in Brazil to see children walking alone, even by the side of a busy road late at night. The sight would have been more alarming for Dean, who'd only been in the country for a few days; but few Brazilians, I imagined, would have paid her a moment's glance.

I don't know what made me turn around and go back. Everything inside me told me there was nothing sinister about what we'd just seen, that she was just a young country girl making her way back home. I saw a broken gap in the central reservation, checked behind me and swung round onto the other side.

Even as we drove another half a mile back up the motorway to find somewhere to turn around, I fully expected not to find her there again. But there she was, at almost the same spot, meandering along in the same way, her eyes fixed on the ground as if ashamed of the spotlight lighting her up every few seconds. This time I indicated and slowed down, and she immediately changed direction and walked straight towards us.

I rolled down the window and she peered inside.

"Hi… you're not doing 'programmes', are you?" I asked. I never liked the phrase – it made paying a person for sex seem like a perfectly acceptable transaction.

"Yeah," she replied softly, her bony elbows now resting on our window-frame. Even up close, the tiny girl's body was skeletal, emaciated, her sunken eyes big in a gaunt face. She began tugging at the car's rear-door handle. "Let me in," she said, "before anyone sees."

"No, no. We just want to speak to you. I'll just pull in over there."

That this child was quite willing to get into a car with two strangers, on a dark motorway at 1.30 in the morning, within seconds of us pulling up, is something I will never get over.

We got out of the car to speak to her. She was guarded at first, folding her arms tightly around her body, her eyes betraying the shy innocence of a child. She didn't say much, but what she did say revealed a life of almost unimaginable tragedy. Her name was Leilah, she told us. She said she was fourteen, although she looked younger. She lived with her mother, father, and four siblings just beyond the overgrown wasteland behind us. Every night she came to the motorway to offer her body for sale to the truck drivers. But she never sold herself short, she said – she wouldn't do it for less than 25 reals (£10) a time. The irony was lost on her – it was how much she thought she was worth.

"Where are your parents?" I asked.

"My mum and dad are at home. They know what I'm doing. When I get home I give them the money I make and they go and buy food. They don't stay up for me. They must be asleep by now."

I asked what happened after a truck driver picked her up. "When he's finished he throws me out," she said. "Sometimes they let me climb down, or sometimes they just kick me out onto the concrete. It's a long way down. That's how I got these." She lifted up her arms to reveal recently healed scars on her elbows.

Suddenly a huge car-carrier truck thundered past us, blaring its horn and deliberately screeching its air brakes menacingly. It jolted Leilah out of her train of thought. "I need to get back. Is there anything else you want?"

I thought for a moment. My heart was breaking for this young girl, who I knew I would probably never meet again after tonight. I placed my hand gently on her shoulder and tried to catch her eye. "Just to tell you... that you're worth much more than you could ever imagine. Please, Leilah, go back home, don't do this any more. You deserve much, much more."

It was the first time that Leilah managed a smile. It was probably the moment she realized we didn't want to use her like all the other men who shuddered to a halt beside that crumbling concrete verge. She even offered out her arms for a hug. Then she turned around and sauntered back along the motorway, dwarfed and silhouetted by the blinding yellow headlights hurtling towards her. We watched as she walked back into the night, finally disappearing into the haze of dust and diesel fumes.

Our encounter with Leilah had lasted less than five minutes, but it had changed everything. Dean would later say that it had been a turning point in his life: "It broke my heart that a little girl was out there in the darkness, wandering around in her own nightmare. It made me want to enter that nightmare, to do anything to bring her out of it," he wrote.

The worst part was having to just stand by as a vulnerable child, whom you instinctively wanted to protect, just walked off into another horrific night of sexual abuse and violence. She would soon be at the mercy of some filthy truck driver, and would probably end up thrown like a rag doll onto the hard tarmac – while we were sleeping peacefully in our hotel beds. Just the thought made us both feel sick to the stomach.

Leilah's tragic existence wasn't the only thing that was causing the anger to boil up inside. Just that morning Dean and I had met with the president of the state assembly, the second most powerful person, after the governor, in Minas Gerais state. We told him we were heading out to the BR-116 motorway to investigate child prostitution, and he laughed dismissively. "You're wasting your time," he told us. "You won't find a thing. Yes, there used to be a problem, but Brazil has moved on – that kind of thing doesn't happen any more." What chance did a girl like Leilah have if even those who had the power to do something to help her refused to believe she even existed?

It was Dean who eventually broke the silence, thumping the dashboard with his fist.

"How can anyone let that happen?" he fumed. "She's just a child. I never thought… I mean, to read about it is one thing, it breaks your heart. But to see it, to see this?…" He cursed under his breath. "How could anyone do that to a girl like her?"

Dean pulled at his hair with the same fist as tears blurred his eyes and welled to their brink. I knew what he was feeling – those raw emotions, the anger, the helplessness. I'd gone through them too, wept and sometimes cursed, as I'd seen for myself the evil done to the "least of these" – young, innocent girls, voiceless and powerless, sold for a fistful of coins.

Dean immediately apologized for his language. He scrubbed his face with his hand and laughed at his fiery outburst. Then we both stared ahead in silence as we drove onwards, through the deserted town centre to our hotel.

\* \* \*

The place where we had met Leilah was almost unrecognizable in the light of day. Last night's gloomy backdrop of blackness revealed itself as a squalid mishmash of tin-roofed shacks, rising up a steep dirt hillside. Further up, in the direction where she had wandered off, the metal towers of a sprawling electricity substation rose up into a cloudless sky. Opposite, beside a petrol station forecourt and truck repair yard, there was a row of seedy motels – Dreams, Paloma, La Pointe – their illuminated signs still flickering on and off.

The traffic was also much more intense in the day. Everywhere you looked there were transport trucks manoeuvring, kicking up clouds of dust and spewing out thick black fumes. The traffic hurtling along the motorway was constant, roaring like an angry river, leaving our eyes stinging and our ears ringing.

We had parked on the petrol station forecourt and dashed across the motorway to the spot where, ten hours earlier, we had talked to young Leilah. The sun, almost directly above us, scorched the backs of our necks. As I looked around Dean was pacing up and down, lost in thought, his eyes fixed on the ground, where our footprints were still visible in the dusty red earth. Both of us had spent a restless night struggling with what we had seen, but Dean had said little since we'd met for breakfast. Eventually he looked at me.

"What if there are more Leilahs? Last night, she was just one girl, and even then we almost didn't see her. This motorway is thousands of miles long. There could be hundreds, thousands more. Don't we need to find out?"

Dean and I intended to make a brief visit to Governador Valadares, spending just one night there. We'd left our wives, and my seven-month-old son, waiting at a friend's house in another town seventy miles away. From there, we'd planned to drive down to the Rio de Janeiro coast and spend our last few days in Brazil lazing on a sun-soaked beach. If we were to go further, we'd have to change all our plans. But Dean was right. For some reason we'd been allowed a glimpse into one girl's living nightmare. The least this demanded of us was to look further, to discover what was really going on, to find out if there was anything we could do to help.

I thought for a while, then turned to Dean: "There are no more large towns for hundreds of miles. I only know one place, a little town called Medina. It's along the edge of the motorway. I passed by there once before, but I only stayed for half an hour. I always wanted to find out more. What do you think?"

I didn't need to wait for an answer: he was already standing at the side of the motorway, waiting for a chance to cross. It was 11.30 a.m. when we left Governador Valadares, taking the BR-116 northwards. We would be on the same road for another six and a half hours. It would be a journey that would change our lives forever.

## Chapter 2

# Keep Going

The sun was already dipping under the hills as our road-weary wheels finally shuddered over Medina's dusty cobbled streets.

It was 6 p.m. and as we arrived in the town's main square, shopkeepers were already pulling down their shutters and bringing in their wares. The square was still bustling, though. Women laden with bags and trailing children criss-crossed the busy street, while groups of men wearing frayed straw hats played cards on the pavement or sat idly on the square's whitewashed walls. Some tracked us with their eyes as we circled round, clearly unused to seeing an unfamiliar face roll up in town.

Medina was nothing like the town we'd left that morning. Governador Valadares was an industrial hub, a sprawling urban mass and the kind of place where you'd expect to find serious social ills. Medina, on the other hand, was just a tiny rural community. We began to wonder if our long journey had been for nothing, if we'd been wrong in thinking that what we'd seen in last night's polluted edge of town might also be a problem in a slow, backwater place like this.

We knew no one here, and because our decision to come here had been so unexpected, I hadn't tried to contact anyone who might have been able to help us. We decided to find the local children's council, the government unit which deals with child welfare cases, and which is normally the most informed about the local situation with children at risk. But by the time we arrived at their offices, we found that they too had shut for the day. We stood there for a while, our legs still aching from the long car ride, wondering what we should do, and if this simple country town even had a place where we could stay overnight.

"You looking for Rita?" asked a withered old man trudging up the hill in overworn flip-flops.

"No, no. We were wanting to speak to someone from the children's council, that's all," I replied.

"Then that'll be Rita," he insisted. "The children's councillor. She lives in that road over there."

He waved a bony arm beyond a row of flaking painted houses on the opposite side of the street. There, a group of women separating corn kernels on a doorstep directed us further up to a row of uneven terraced cottages. Another man leaning out of his wooden window-frame pointed to a bright lilac wall opposite. I rang the doorbell and we waited as a metal gate rattled open.

Rita was a tall, olive-skinned woman with cascading brown hair and a wide, friendly smile. She offered her hand before we'd even managed to introduce ourselves.

"I'm so sorry to disturb you at home," I said. "I'm a journalist from England... and this is Dean, he's a country singer from Canada." Rita nodded as if it was the kind of sentence she heard every day. "We're trying to find out more about issues affecting children in Medina. I wondered if..."

"Well, don't just stand there," she said without hesitation. "Come on in."

Dean and I were soon sitting down on a sofa in Rita's living room, slightly bewildered at our totally unguarded welcome, while our host rattled around in her kitchen. She emerged a few minutes later with a freshly brewed flask of coffee and a plateful of *beijú*, a sweet biscuit made from tapioca flour. She sat down opposite us as I tried again to explain why we'd suddenly turned up unannounced at her front door.

"Rita, last night we met a young girl selling her body on the motorway. We decided to find out more. I don't really know why we ended up coming here to Medina. I wondered if you might be able to help us…"

This time, Rita looked startled and the smile suddenly fell from her face. For a moment I wondered if we'd offended her by even suggesting that such a thing could happen in her small country town.

Then she composed herself, leaned towards us and began.

"I don't know how you arrived here, I don't know how you even heard about this town, but… I think you must be angels sent by God."

Rita's voice trembled with emotion as she told us of a tragedy almost too horrific to grasp: of hundreds of girls forced by their own families into a life of humiliation and abuse; of mothers who swapped their own daughters for a bag of beans or a packet of cigarettes; of girls aged twelve and thirteen who were dying of AIDS; and many more, she said, whose fate she didn't know, whom she had cared for but who had one day climbed into a truck heading north or south along the BR-116 and never returned home.

"The situation's so desperate," said Rita. "These girls, we're losing them all the time. Every week I hear of another who's gone, disappeared up the motorway. It's like a handful of earth that's falling through your fingers, and you can't do anything but watch it fall. As much as I try, I can't stop them from falling."

Tears streamed down Rita's face as the pain she had been keeping inside for so long welled up and flooded out. Every day she'd cried to God for help, she told us. The last few days were the worst, when she wondered if she could carry on facing this huge disaster alone. Next to me, Dean was in tears too. I hadn't translated anything that Rita had said – there just wasn't time – but he knew, he could see her grief, the desperation and heartbreak etched on her face.

Child prostitution, Rita explained, was simply a way of life in Medina. No one was shocked to see a twelve-year-old girl standing at the side of the road, advertising her pre-pubescent body for sale. Everybody knew somebody whose young daughter was "working" in a roadside brothel. "Everyone's happy when a baby girl is born," she said, not because of the prospect of their daughter playing with dolls or dressing up, but "because in around a decade, they'll have a valuable source of income."

Dean and I were stunned. We'd come here knowing that we might find something upsetting, but never this. Even if the problem was confined to this small town, we'd still stumbled upon a tragedy of alarming proportions. The words of the president of the state assembly – "You won't find a thing… that kind of thing doesn't happen any more" – once again echoed through our minds; and I thought of other people I knew in Belo Horizonte, the state capital – educated, informed people – who had no idea of what was happening just a day's drive from their front doors.

"But Rita," I said, "this is a scandal! Why doesn't anybody know? Why isn't anybody trying to do something about it?"

Rita leaned forward. "Matt, nobody comes to Medina, apart from truck drivers. There are no tourists, no foreigners, no TV cameras. These girls, they're worth nothing in Brazil, they're forgotten, ignored by everyone. Out of sight, out of mind, and most people would prefer to keep it that way. Would you like to meet some of them?"

\* \* \*

It was already dark by the time we arrived at a shabby brick building set just yards back from the edge of the BR-116. The house would have been invisible in the blackness if it were not for a single, precariously wired bulb hanging above the front door. A makeshift clothes line made from barbed wire, stretched out at neck height, doubled as a menacing warning to keep out.

The house, Rita had explained, belonged to José, a father of four girls aged eight to sixteen. He worked fifty miles away at a granite mine, returning home for a few days every couple of weeks. In the meantime it was his daughters who were the breadwinners, plying their bodies on the motorway and using their own bedrooms as their "workplaces".

José, who happened to be home, hobbled and coughed as he invited us inside. The walls were covered in black mould, and the floor was strewn with blankets, dirty clothes, and unwashed plates. I peered into one of the girls' bedrooms. It was just as filthy as the rest of the house, but still recognizable as the room of a teenage girl. Posters of boy bands hung on the walls, a plastic picture frame covered in love-hearts was propped up on a bedside table, and a collection of furry toy animals had been neatly placed at the top of the bed.

"Are Viviane and Sâmia at home?" Rita asked. They were the middle two girls, aged twelve and fourteen.

"No, they went to church," replied José immediately.

I gave Rita a puzzled look. "That's what they always say," she said, under her breath. "They think it will get them off the hook when the children's councillor drops by."

It wasn't long until the two girls appeared, and they certainly weren't dressed for church, with heavy make-up and skimpy, figure-hugging dresses. They became sheepish as they caught sight of Rita, and although they told her they had just gone for a *rolé* – a wander around – you could tell they knew there wasn't much point trying to fool her.

The dark-skinned girls looked older than they were, but there were occasional glimpses of the children they really were: a shy smile, an awkward turn of phrase. They arrived home linking each other's arms, and didn't let go for the whole time we were with them.

We stood on the motorway's edge, our conversation being drowned out by a truck roaring by every few seconds, shaking the ground beneath us. I tried to imagine ever getting a moment's sleep in one of those musty bedrooms just yards away. For those young girls, though, the rooms were much worse, a nightmare they could never escape from, a constant reminder of the indignity and abuse they suffered day in, day out. Even the beds they slept in were the scenes of countless loveless, violent encounters, which one by one had gradually stolen away their innocence.

We left that dark, oppressive place with Viviane and Sâmia assuring us they were going inside and straight to bed, but when we looked back, the girls were already heading back to the motorway, disappearing into the darkness, their arms still tightly linked.

From the edge of the BR-116 it was a short distance to the home of twelve-year-old Letícia. Along the way Rita provided us with a tragic commentary: "See that house over there? It was a brothel which specialized in underage girls. We got it shut down but it reopened a few months later... and that petrol station over there? The other week I found a girl of eleven climbing into a truck. A driver had promised her he'd take her to the beach in Porto Seguro."

Letícia lived in another of the brightly painted terraced cottages that we had seen all over Medina, in a district called Várzea Grande. The area, according to Rita, was crawling with violent drug gangs, and was often the scene of gruesome gangland murders. Letícia's house, however, was different to the one we'd just come from. It was poor but clean and tidy; pictures hung from the walls, a rug was placed neatly on the floor. Her father, Armando, had neatly combed hair and was smartly dressed in a pair of trousers and a long-sleeved shirt.

It soon became clear that the problem in this house was very different to the last, but no less tragic. Armando was a churchgoer, and a devoted, well-meaning father who just wanted the best for his daughter. But, to his horror, he had found himself caught up in Medina's child prostitution nightmare. His dark eyes and haggard face betrayed the torment of a man who was desperately trying to prevent his precious little girl from being wrenched away from him.

"I don't know what to do, I hardly sleep at night," he told us. "Letícia used to be such a good girl. She was always at church, she even sang in the choir. She's only twelve! I worry so much, it's making me sick – just thinking about what might be happening to her out there."

It was a year ago, he told us, when Letícia had been to see her mother, who lived in São Paulo, Brazil's biggest city. Letícia had longed to see her mother again, but when she got there something happened – her father didn't know what – which caused her to run away from home. The next morning police found her, unconscious, lying in a ditch. She had been raped.

He remembered: "It started after that. She was different from the moment she got home. I would find her sleeping underneath her bed, or on the water tank on the roof of the house. Then she started running away, mixing with the wrong crowd and getting into trouble. I turn around and suddenly she's gone.

"It's killing me. I don't sleep, I don't even go to bed, I just stand on my doorstep waiting for her to come home. She can see what it's doing to me, but it doesn't stop her doing it."

While her father was looking anxiously down the road for his lost daughter, Letícia was on the BR-116, jumping into truckers' cabins, wandering around dark lorry parks and petrol station forecourts, allowing herself to be used and abused in exchange for a fistful of reals. One violent night at the hands of a gang of rapists – none of which had been caught – had taken away every last scrap of her self-esteem, and the young girl now seemed intent on self-destruction. One night she'd been found 100 miles away from Medina, in a brothel bedroom with a 55-year-old man. Another time police had brought her home after an older prostitute in a town in the next state north had stabbed her with a broken bottle in a fight. Her father recounted each fact with a trembling voice, as if he himself didn't believe the story he was telling.

It was then that Letícia appeared – a small, pale-skinned girl with shoulder-length brown hair pulled back in a pigtail. She trudged unwillingly into the room and slumped down between Dean and me on the sofa, fixing her eyes on the floor and holding her folded arms defensively to her chest.

"Letícia, these people are wanting to help girls like you, and wanted to come and see you," said Rita sympathetically.

Letícia grunted and shrugged her shoulders.

I tried. "Why do you run away? Your father seems so worried about you," I said. She pouted her mouth and said nothing.

I tried again. "Is there anything that would stop you running away?"

"Dunno."

"If you could be anyone in life, who would you be…?"

Letícia gave an embarrassed smile and murmured, "I want to be a lawyer." It was a subject that, for a few brief seconds, brought her out of her shell as we told her to hold on to her dream, that she could be all she wanted to be.

Armando sat in the corner, beaming with love at every clumsy word his daughter spoke. We couldn't begin to imagine his torment, knowing that soon she would probably be back on a dark motorway shoulder, offering herself to the next stranger who appeared on the horizon.

It was hard to leave them both as we said goodbye, and we promised to do what we could to help.

The last home Rita took us to was the most difficult to get to, at the top of a steep, rocky hill at the far edge of the town. We finally arrived at a low mud-brick house standing eerily between two huge black boulders. The place was in complete darkness; none of the houses had electricity. The only light was the glow from a cigarette held between the fingers of a thin, beady-eyed woman crouching beside a rotting wooden fence. Her name was Maria, and she was the mother of Mariana, a thirteen-year-old girl who Rita had been trying to help since she was nine.

Rita asked if Mariana was at home. "Oh, she's not here, she went to church," replied her mother, taking a final puff on the cigarette butt before flicking it away. This time I was wiser – and besides, it was nearly eleven o'clock at night. We told her we'd come back the next morning.

As we drove back to Medina's town square, and our *pousada* (guest house) for the night, Rita filled us in on Mariana's story.

"Both her mother and her grandmother started as prostitutes at a young age, so of course Mariana was simply expected to do the same. She's never known anything else. For these people, sending their daughter off for her first 'programme' is as normal as her playing with her first Barbie doll."

\* \* \*

Mariana's mother probably never expected us to be back there at 8.30 the next morning, but she invited us inside, apologizing repeatedly for the mess as she shooed away the scrawny dogs and cleared a space on an old, tattered sofa.

The building was filled with smoke which poured from an open fire boiling water in the kitchen. She was making pasta soup for lunch, she said – only she didn't have any pasta, just some rotting chicken feet she'd scavenged from the market waste. The walls were stained black with soot, and the floor was littered with tattered clothes, broken toys, and cigarette ends. On a wooden stand there was an old TV and a video recorder – probably to make it look as if the house had an electricity supply.

Maria was thin and gaunt, and trembled as she ripped a page from an exercise book, cut off a slice of tobacco, and rolled a cigarette. She sent her young son to call her daughter, who she said was at a neighbour's house, and minutes later Mariana appeared, out of breath, at the front door. She had a child's face and an innocent smile.

Perhaps more than any of the girls we'd met so far, Mariana reminded me of thirteen-year-old girls I knew back home. She was lively and wide-eyed, interested in what we had to say and excited at having a Canadian singer in her house. She showed us a poster of her heart-throb, Justin Bieber – and melted when Dean said Justin was from Canada also. Then she dashed off to fetch her notebook, filled with girly poems, scribbled flowers and love-hearts.

But as Rita began to talk to her about the harsh reality of her life, she became quiet, and her brown eyes began filling up with tears and sadness. At one point Rita went into another room with her mother, and Mariana turned to me and whispered: "I hate it here. It's my mum. She drinks. She doesn't treat me like a mum should treat her daughter. It makes me want to run away and never come back."

We didn't know it yet, but Mariana's life was more awful than even Rita realized. A month after we left she would discover the truth – that Mariana's mother and grandmother were forcing her to sell her body to truck drivers on the motorway. Sometimes Maria would even walk her down there herself, negotiate her price and take the money she made, or send her to a roadside brothel with instructions to return with money – or face a severe beating.

Although we didn't know the whole story, both Dean and I had been deeply affected by meeting Mariana. There was something about her – a deep sense of loneliness and longing in her eyes. We left there feeling shattered, knowing that all she needed was the simple chance to be a normal, care-free teenager – something most girls take for granted, but which for her seemed like the most distant of dreams.

\*\*\*

From Mariana's home we dropped Rita back at the children's council and headed out of town, taking the BR-116 for the long journey back to Governador Valadares, Rio de Janeiro, and home – me to Britain, Dean to Canada.

Behind us, the town shrank and finally vanished, but the stories we'd heard, the girls we'd met, were growing louder and bigger. Our minds were spinning. How could it be possible –

so much tragedy, so much injustice, so many accomplices to so much evil? And Medina was just one small town out of thousands along this vast, 2,800-mile-long motorway.

The potential size of this scandal was almost too huge to get our heads around – and yet nobody knew about it, not 500 miles away in the state capital, and certainly not many thousands more miles away in Canada or England. Most of its victims were just young girls, a little over a decade into life, yet already lost, their lives broken, their self-esteem completely shattered.

We were already driving through undulating green hills when Dean eventually turned to me. "What are we going to do?" he asked. "Whatever you decide, I'm with you, man."

I was already thinking hard. I had a good job, a young family, a mortgage. My days of being radical, of acting on impulse, were over. Yet everything inside me was telling me I should do something reckless for these poor young girls – whatever it might take to bring this tragedy to light, and to bring them hope. Tears welled up in my eyes as God's love for the lost girls of this obscure Brazilian motorway began to overwhelm me.

"Forget what the world considers precious," he seemed to say. "Nothing is more precious to me than these little ones."

We need to keep going, I thought. If there were more girls trapped in the same nightmare, we had to find them, shout out about them, do something to save them. We couldn't just stop here and go home. We had to keep going.

*Chapter 3*

# The Journey Begins

N one of what you will read in this book would have happened if we hadn't come across Leilah on that muggy January night. If we'd never caught sight of her, or if we hadn't turned around to try to find her again, we wouldn't have carried on to Medina, and probably would have returned to our countries to continue as normal with our busy lives. Those lives were about as far removed from that remote, sun-cracked motorway as you could get.

I'm a journalist, and at the time I was in my eighth year as a feature writer for the British newspaper, the *Daily Mirror*. My world was the shiny towers of Canary Wharf, the money-drenched business district of London, the leafy green of the Royal Borough of Greenwich, and the packed subway stations, double-decker buses, and every other sight and sound in between. Hired as a fresh-faced journalism graduate by Piers Morgan (now a US chat show host), I had quickly become used to the high-pressure life of a tabloid newspaper newsroom, where I could be despatched to the other side of the world at a moment's notice, be sent to a posh London hotel to interview a famous celebrity, or go undercover on a "secret squirrel" assignment. And I could be asked to do almost anything for a tabloid stunt, like singing "I Dreamed a Dream" outside Susan Boyle's front door to see how many hits I would get on YouTube, walking around the Houses of Parliament in a life-like bear costume, or trying to fillet a fish on *Masterchef* under the disapproving eye of Michel Roux Jr. I would arrive at work every morning not knowing where I would end up, how I might end up looking, or even if I would be back home at the end of the day.

I'd already lived in Brazil, working with girls living on the streets of Belo Horizonte, one of the country's biggest cities. I'd gone there after university, moved by the suffering of abandoned children, but soon realized that one group – the girls – wasn't being catered for. We set up a project called Meninadança – literally, "girl dance" – using dance to reach out to street girls, with a house in the city centre where they could go during the day, and eventually residential homes where the girls could leave the streets for good. The dance was effective in helping the girls discover their worth and potential for themselves, and ended up helping many to leave the streets for good. But I'd left Brazil nearly a decade ago, and although that experience never left me, it had become a memory, a post-uni adventure that many of us have before getting stuck into the "real" world of work.

Dean Brody's world was even further removed from that obscure Brazilian highway. A rising star of country music in his native Canada, he was used to playing to crowds of thousands, being feted by TV cameras and radio stations, and managing the affections of a growing army of fans. His first single was a Top 40 hit in both Canada and the United States; he'd just been nominated for five of Canada's biggest music awards, and, as we were driving along that dusty Brazilian highway, his latest single had been at number one in the Canadian charts for a month.

Dean had grown up in a ranching town, population 850, in the foothills of the Rocky Mountains, where he met his wife, Iris, and where, like most boys there, he'd started working at the local sawmill, aged fifteen. At night he'd sit under the stars, sing songs on an old guitar, and dream of one day seeing his name in lights. He was twenty-six when he and Iris finally went after that dream, packed a trailer with all their belongings and drove the 2,000 miles south to Nashville, Tennessee. Being in the home of country music helped, but it was Dean's powerful voice and song-writing talent that, four years later, got him his first recording contract.

He had never been to Brazil before, but since their small-town days he and Iris had always felt a special concern for young girls caught up in prostitution and human trafficking around the world. A Christian with a heart for the poor and vulnerable, he had once considered working abroad with children in need himself, but eventually made a difficult decision to concentrate on his singing and song-writing. As his career began to take off, Dean made a promise to himself that, if success were to come his way, he would use it to do something that might make a difference. It was a promise he never forgot.

Our paths first crossed in March 2010 – the start of a close friendship and an extraordinary journey. My wife, Dani, and I had just moved house and we were expecting our first child. It was time to settle down, feather the nest, concentrate on family. Little did we know that our lives were about to take an entirely different turn.

The reason was a book I'd written seven years earlier, *Remember Me, Rescue Me*, the story of an unforgettable and eye-opening journey around Brazil. With my visa about to expire and a place at journalism college already confirmed, I'd decided to spend my last months there travelling around the country, looking further at the issue of child prostitution – a problem we'd begun to encounter more frequently in working with Belo Horizonte's street girls. What I found was heartbreaking: girls as young as eleven caught up in a grotesque trade which seemed to be present in every corner of that vast country, from tourist destinations such as Recife and Fortaleza to remote mining towns in the Amazon jungle.

The journey lasted five months and covered over 5,000 miles, after which there was only enough time to catch a plane back home, move to London, and start my journalism studies at City University. I wrote up the book between lectures, delivered the manuscript to the publisher, and got stuck into life in an entirely different world – a world of scoops, deadlines, and often long breaking-news days. Before I knew it, the tragic girls I'd met during that harrowing trip had become mere memories, and the book had been years out of print.

Little did I know it, but thousands of miles away across the Atlantic, Dean Brody had found a copy of that book and was reading it for the first time, feeling the same mix of horror and heartache as I had when I'd written it. He got to the last page during a flight to Nashville to record his second album, one that would top the Canadian charts. Fighting tears from his eyes as he closed the book, he decided to try to make contact with me.

At the end of a busy day of working, then preparing for the imminent arrival of our baby, I sat down at my computer and noticed an email sitting unopened in my inbox.

"Hi Matt, My name is Dean Brody," it started. He explained how he and Iris had always wanted to help children involved in prostitution, but didn't know even where to start. So they started scouring the internet, trying to find out more about the issue. He went on:

**It was surprising to me that Brazil had such a problem and was ranked among the worst. Then I came across your book and it broke my heart.**

So began an exchange of emails between two strangers who, on paper at least, were as different as you could get: me, an English journalist and music graduate from a sheltered upbringing in an unremarkable Nottinghamshire town; he a Canadian country boy from the Rocky Mountains who'd spent his youth hunting, fishing, and chopping up wood. But we soon discovered we had much more in common, and the more we talked, the more I recognized my own thoughts and passions – that same sense of urgency that had driven me years earlier when we'd rushed to rescue abandoned, crack-addicted girls from the big-city streets.

Five months after that first email, Dean, Iris, and I arranged to meet in Brazil. The idea was to introduce Dean and Iris to Brazil, get to know one another and see where, if anywhere, they could get involved. I knew of a school headteacher in Belo Horizonte who was working with young people from a local *favela*, and I thought I could link them up.

After a twelve-hour flight from Heathrow, I arrived at Rio de Janeiro's international airport at 11.30 p.m., anxious to finally meet Dean and Iris – but instead I got a distraught email as soon as I switched on my phone:

**Matt, we were turned away at the airport… it never crossed our minds that Canadians might need a visa to enter Brazil! I'm so sorry. I felt sick when I called and realized you were already on the plane to Rio.**

Disappointed but still pleased to be back in Brazil, I spent the week catching up with old friends.

It was three months later when we finally met, this time on Canadian soil. Dani, our son Milo – now aged four months – and I spent a week with Dean, Iris, and their two young children at their home overlooking the Atlantic Ocean in Nova Scotia. Within hours of meeting we felt as if we had known each other for years. Dean was unassuming and soft-spoken, just the opposite of what you might expect of a country music star. Iris was bubbly and chatty and immediately hit it off with Dani. We spent the week sitting in coffee shops, walking by the sea, and playing football – English and Canadian – on Dean's lawn, while endlessly talking and planning what we could do to try to help exploited girls in Brazil.

We decided to found charities, one in England and one in Canada, to raise funds which we could use to support existing projects in the country. The first would be the *favela* project in Belo Horizonte which was helping to stop teenage girls falling into a life of prostitution and gangs.

Three months later, we all met again in Brazil, this time as close friends. During the first week we visited the project in Belo Horizonte and attended an evening inauguration ceremony, where Dean sang. He had also wanted to visit one of the places I had described in my book, so the next day – after a meeting with the state assembly president – we set off eastwards. The nearest town to where we were going was Governador Valadares, a seven-hour drive. So it was that, in the early hours of the next morning, we found ourselves approaching the town's scruffy outskirts, and happened upon a young girl who would change our lives.

Our encounter with Leilah affected both of us more deeply than we even realized at the time. Dean later wrote to his fans:

**I had never seen it. I had read about it, talked about it, and wanted to do something about it, but to see it up close was another thing altogether, and it busted me up.**

Our short trip to Medina was similarly life-changing. I had arrived there prepared for the possibility of being shocked, but I had never expected the immensity of the tragedy we found. The situation was bigger, darker, than anything we had ever imagined – bigger even than the problem of street children I had once tried to fight – and caught in the middle were countless lost and entirely unprotected young lives.

After being reunited with our wives, we spent our last few days in Brazil talking, researching, and planning our next steps. We were well aware that, after a few weeks back home, what we had seen and heard in a remote corner of this vast country would seem like a dream, something which could easily fade as the pressures of work and family life took over. But we were determined not to forget, or lose the sense of urgency, that overwhelming feeling that we would "do anything to bring them out of it". We wanted to part with a definite plan.

We pledged that we would return as soon as we could, and continue our journey north up the BR-116, over 1,500 miles to the end of the motorway at the city of Fortaleza on the north-east coast of Brazil. The highway would take us through some of the remotest parts of the country – isolated, often lawless places punished by drought and grinding poverty. Along the way we would investigate, dig deep, document what we found, try to find out what was really going on and, if needed, do what we could to bring this tragedy out of the shadows. In the meantime we would continue raising money, supporting projects that we felt were helping girls in Brazil who were at risk of being exploited in prostitution or trafficking.

I knew, though, that there was a bigger decision that I had to make. I would achieve little being thousands of miles away, and particularly if I were still living a manic existence in a stressful, life-consuming job. The thought of leaving a position I was proud of − that buzzing, national newspaper environment I thrived on − filled me with trepidation. My wife Dani is Brazilian, but she had grown used to living in London and had never imagined she would ever return to her home country to live, especially with us having just started a family. She too was full of contradicting emotions, worries, and reservations as over the next few days we considered leaving behind the places and people to which we had grown attached, uprooting and moving to the other side of the world.

By the time Dani and I had bid farewell to Dean and Iris at Rio's international airport, boarding our own plane bound for home a few hours later, our minds were made up. We would spend the rest of the year preparing to move to Brazil. With three months to go, I would hand in my notice at the *Daily Mirror*, and to support us once we were there I would work as a freelance journalist, and see if I could make a living sending stories from Brazil back to the British newspapers. Still, it didn't make us feel any less nervy. I had always been a staffer and I had no idea if trying my hand at freelancing would pay the bills. That little ache in the pit of my stomach stayed with me pretty much constantly for most of the coming months.

\* \* \*

A few weeks after arriving back, Dean called me:

"Matt, I got home and wrote a song about Leilah. I just sat down and it flowed out. Let me know what you think."

The song was a haunting, heartfelt ballad which brought the memories of our journey, and that first encounter with the girl in the lilac dress, flooding back. It became the soundtrack to the next nine months as we prepared to return, travelling round churches and friends telling them about our plans:

> **Blinding headlights, the smell of the black**
>   **diesel fumes,**
> **It ain't no life for a child as innocent as you.**
> **You're a lamb among lions,**
> **They take your diamonds and toss you to**
>   **the side of a lonely road in the rain,**
> **And you stand there, torn like a rag doll**
> **As tears streak your face.**
>
> **Leilah, oh Leilah, you're a beautiful girl,**
> **Precious wild flower of Brazil.**
> **Oh Leilah, oh Leilah, the world has forgot**
>   **you,**
> **But I know that I never will.**

The urgent need was never far from our minds, especially as I kept in regular contact with Rita, the children's councillor from Medina. Every time I called her, the situation seemed to have worsened, with more young girls getting caught up. Of particular concern was Mariana, the thirteen-year-old Justin Bieber fan whose mother had forced her into a life of prostitution on the motorway. Rita discovered she had run away from her home, and for weeks no one knew where she was.

Eventually we got news. "The police raided a brothel about fifty miles away from here," she told me. "They found Mariana in bed with another twelve-year-old girl and an older man. A woman was there too, their pimp. Matt, she's in over her head now. It looks like she's already been recruited by a prostitution ring. I think we've lost her. I don't know what to do."

I remembered that bright-eyed young girl whose hopes and dreams still seemed intact, but who desperately wanted to get away from the cold-hearted mother who was cruelly exploiting her. We sent a friend from Belo Horizonte, who had been a "substitute mother" to the street girls we'd worked with previously, to try to take her away. But Mariana's mother and grandmother stubbornly refused to let her go – after all, she was a source of income, a precious "commodity". That night, Dani spent the night in tears, her heart breaking for this girl trapped in abuse and exploitation, prevented from finding help by those who were supposed to love her.

As time went on, Mariana's situation went from bad to worse. Weeks later, we heard that she had disappeared again. When she finally reappeared, she'd discovered she was pregnant. Once again, we sent the same friend to try to take her out of there, but again she met with resistance, this time in the form of threats from the local drug dealers, who told her never to come back. As she returned once more, on her own, to Belo Horizonte, the friend called me:

"It was her grandmother who called the drugs gang. She's the one who calls the shots, and she's decided she won't ever let Mariana go."

Three months before we were due to leave, as planned, I handed in my notice, and we began to sell or give away almost everything we had – furniture, books, CDs, cutlery, pots and pans – until we had just about enough to fit into four suitcases. On my last day at work my colleagues threw a leaving do, and presented me with my own framed *Daily Mirror* front page. The headline was "From Here to Matternity", remembering the time I had to dress up as a pregnant man and walk around the streets of London to report people's reactions. There was also a picture of me wearing a suit, hiding in a bush with David Attenborough, with the great man saying: "You're not really dressed for the Brazilian rainforest, Matt."

On our last night, eighteen-month-old Milo slept with his Nana – she had often looked after him as we travelled around the country, and they had grown close. We got up at 4 a.m. to leave for the airport, and my mum couldn't hold back the tears as she said goodbye and let go of the grandson she knew she wouldn't see for months. Several hours later, we were waiting on the runway, hearts in our mouths, anxious, nervous, expectant, but ready to go.

## Chapter 4

# Looking for Leilah

"**M**y, my, young man, I never thought I'd see you again! What are you doing here?"

Abigail held out her arms and I gave her a tight hug. We hadn't seen each other for nearly ten years, but we went back a long way. We'd got to know each other during the years I worked with street girls in Belo Horizonte, the state capital, when Abigail, from Governador Valadares, was the head of the town's children's council. She had also helped me when I had visited Valadares researching for my book *Remember Me, Rescue Me*, taking me on police raids to brothels and strip joints, and introducing me to the "one ninety-nine girls", the children so-called because they would sell their bodies for a handful of centavos.

It had been nearly three months since I'd arrived with my family in Brazil. Our move had been effortful, although not more so than we'd expected. Beginning our lives again virtually from scratch, we'd started with our identity documents, then found a place to live, bought furniture, opened bank accounts, found day care for Milo, and a hundred other things we'd never thought needed to be done, but were close to feeling at home again.

I'd also begun my work as a freelance journalist, and thankfully, it was working out. Almost every day I was getting something published in a newspaper back home. So far I'd written about everything from a soccer star accidentally shooting a woman in the hand, to a baby being born with two heads, and even a man who was caught at a Brazilian airport with 200 live fish stuffed in his suitcase.

Dean had found a space in his own hectic schedule and had flown out so we could continue our journey up the BR-116. We decided to start back in Governador Valadares, the town where we had come across little Leilah, and work our way northwards. For the last year that young girl had been on Dean's mind, even as he toured Canada, played the fame game at award ceremonies and made TV and radio appearances. "Sitting in my hotel, wondering where Leilah is tonight," he'd sometimes email. And the more he thought about her, the more he wanted to find her again, and maybe even find a way of helping her.

I knew that if anyone could help us locate Leilah again, it would be Abigail, so as soon as we arrived back in Valadares we drove round to her house. I immediately noticed, though, how different she seemed to the strong, energetic woman I remembered. She was now older, thinner, more fragile. She had battled throat cancer, she told us. She no longer produced saliva, so had to constantly sip water, and she was under doctor's orders to not get involved in the social work that had once consumed her life. It wouldn't stop her helping us, though, she said, as she got ready to come out.

As she directed us out of the maze of dusty streets towards the BR-116 motorway, I asked Abigail if she missed working at the children's council. Her answer came as a shock.

"Oh, I'd grown weary of that place a long time before the cancer came along."

"But… that was your passion. What could have taken that away?"

"Politics, Matt. The politicians started telling us how to do our work, what we should and shouldn't interfere in. I tried to carry on anyway, but then something happened and I knew I had to get out."

Abigail explained how she and her colleagues had come across an organized child prostitution racket involving the foreign tourists who visit the town for hang-gliding competitions. Valadares is actually the world capital of hang-gliding and its famous Ibituruna Peak, a 4,000-foot-high plug of volcanic rock, is the site of the sport's annual world championships. The children's council was about to move in and make arrests when an order arrived from high up on the town council.

"They told us to leave well alone, to not interfere with child prostitution involving gliders or spectators," Abigail explained. "Someone actually took me aside and said, 'Hang-gliding is the only tourist thing this town has. We can't risk jeopardizing that.' That's when I decided it was time to leave."

With the children's council now firmly in the hands of politicians with other, conflicting interests, the town's child prostitution problem had spiralled out of control, Abigail went on. "There are no more crack-downs, no more police raids. They don't want to bring attention to it, risk generating any bad publicity. I'm sure you'll find it's the same story all the way up this motorway. The powers that be would rather pretend it doesn't happen."

The same thing happened to a friend of hers who had been working with girls at risk in the town's Tourmaline *favela*, continued Abigail. "She discovered that police officers were paying the young girls in her project for sex, so she reported them to the authorities. Nothing happened, and my friend felt so threatened, she ended up having to leave."

The vast Tourmaline *favela* stretched for a mile along the BR-116 on the way out of Valadares, its cheek-by-jowl brick buildings backing right up onto the deafening highway. The slum was the worst in Valadares, a place which made the local newspaper's crime pages on an almost daily basis, a name synonymous with violence, drugs gangs, and appalling social problems. It was also the closest community to the spot on the motorway where we had found Leilah almost a year ago. We decided to begin our search there.

Abigail knew someone who she thought could help us – the owner of a chemist there who, she told us, knew everyone. But after leaving the BR-116 we spent nearly an hour driving round the *favela*'s labyrinthine dirt roads, steep hills, and dead ends, often realizing we were back at a place we'd passed twenty minutes earlier. Abigail, who had come here countless times before, finally admitted she was hopelessly lost, and Dean and I began to wonder how we'd ever manage to locate one, insignificant young girl in a vast, sprawling place like this.

Then, just as we were wondering if we should give up, Abigail suddenly recognized the row of shops she was looking for. Juninho, the chemist, was just arriving back from lunch.

"The young girls who sell their bodies?" he said, a toothpick hanging from the corner of his mouth. "They pass by here every night on their way to the motorway. One of the girls lives just round the corner. Maybe you'll find her there."

We were soon standing in a narrow alleyway, calling through a rotting wooden fence as a pit bull strained against its chain, snarling and snapping at the air. Three girls, of three different sizes, appeared at the door, shovelling food into their mouths from plastic plates. Abigail recognized one of them, Camila, a fourteen-year-old who, she later told us, had regularly been found in prostitution dens and truck parks since she was nine. To us she denied having anything to do with prostitution, but seemed to know an awful lot about the girls who did.

Camila recognized the girl in Dean's iPhone photo as soon as I showed her. "She's always there when we go to the motorway," she said. "You see how tiny she is? The other girls hate her 'cos she gets a lot more work. There are lots of truckers who prefer a skinny little runt like her."

"Do you know where she lives?" I asked.

"No, but she's hardly at home anyway. But I know where she is when she's not inside a truck – behind Mineral Water, that's where you'll find her."

I hadn't a clue what Camila meant by "Mineral Water", but Abigail seemed to understand, so we said our goodbyes and set off. "It's the name of the petrol station, near the place where you met her," she said as we walked back to our car. Getting out of Tourmaline was much easier than finding our way in, and we were soon joining the rushing torrent of trucks, buses, and cars roaring along the BR-116.

On a dirt road behind the "Mineral Water" petrol station, a group of locals confirmed they knew a girl fitting Leilah's description. Her name wasn't Leilah, though – it was Leidiane. She wasn't fifteen as we thought, she was twelve. She had an older sister and a younger brother. And all three could be found there most nights, hunched next to an overgrown pile of bricks on the dark street corner, smoking crack.

"She's completely addicted, poor thing," one woman told us. "When the drugs run out, Leidiane wanders over there to the motorway, or petrol station, does a 'programme' and comes back to buy more. It's tragic."

As I translated to Dean what she was saying, his heart visibly sank. Last year this girl's situation seemed as bad as it could get. But as her true story began to emerge, the reality was worse than we could ever have imagined. "Does she know where they live?" Dean asked.

"I asked her once," the woman replied. "She pointed over there, to the water towers."

Again, Abigail knew where she meant. Dean and I hadn't noticed, but on our way to Tourmaline that morning we'd passed six huge water towers rising up above the urban sprawl. So far it was our only clue to finding Leidiane, so we set off in that direction, making our way along some back streets towards the motorway.

I noticed a skinny young woman, wearing high heels and skimpy shorts, strutting at a pace along the pavement. I pointed her out to Abigail and she agreed: a woman dressed like that could only be a "woman of the night", even though it was only 2 p.m. and the sun was beating down. If she was one of the more experienced girls who turned their trade on the motorway, maybe she could tell us more about Leilah, or Leidiane, as we now knew her. We drove up alongside her and I wound down the window.

Her name was Daiana. She was twenty-five, and surprisingly candid about her life. She was on her way to pick up her two-year-old daughter from her mother's house, she told us. She'd left her while she flagged down truck drivers on the motorway, for which she was deeply ashamed.

"I only do it to feed my habit," she said, leaning her arm on the top of my car. "It's tragic, isn't it? I've got a little girl at home and I'm out here having sex with these disgusting men. And all so I can buy a tiny white rock. Sometimes I even sleep out here on the hard shoulder just so I'm already here when I wake up and need a fix. I'm so messed up!"

We showed her the photo of the girl in the lilac dress.

"Of course I know her – it's Leidiane. I'm always giving her advice when I see her on the road. I tell her to stop doing crack, to go and get help. But she's such a lost little girl. Her mother's got mental problems, she hasn't got anyone in the world.

"She lives behind the third bar on Road Four, over there near the water towers. I hope you'll be able to help her. She'll be dead in a year if you don't, I'm sure of it."

Finally, we had an address of sorts, and had managed to narrow down the town's myriad of streets to a few blocks. But if we thought our search for "Leilah" was nearly over, we were badly mistaken. For the next two hours we drove around in circles, following leads that ended nowhere, clues that turned out to be wrong. First of all, we discovered there wasn't a Road Four anywhere near the water towers. Two girls washing a car on a road nearby told us to try the next street up, where they knew a destitute family lived. There, nobody knew them, but one man was sure a girl fitting Leidiane's description lived a few streets away, at the top of a steep hill.

That road, we discovered, was the fourth street up. A man in a bar at the bottom of the hill also inspected the photo and said he thought the girl lived in a rented shack behind the last bar at the top. By this time, Abigail was getting nervous – the area was a notorious drugs gang territory, and we were now deep inside it. Shifty-looking figures took Dean's iPhone into scruffy bars and showed the girl's photo to their friends. But to our dismay, no one was living behind the bar at the top of the hill, and no one drinking there had ever seen her. It seemed as if we were back to square one.

I noticed that there were some small brick dwellings on the next street up, directly behind the bar, so we decided, as a last attempt, to ask there. But they too were empty. A man washing his car on the road asked what we were doing and we showed him Leidiane's photo.

"Oh, a little girl who wanders around the streets? Yeah, I've seen her. But she doesn't live here, she lives down the bottom, next to the creek."

By now I'd heard enough of locals being sure they knew where the girl lived, and I subtly told him so. "I've nearly finished here. I'll take you there if you like," he replied, turning off his hose.

We followed the man back down the hill, to a dirt track in front of a stinking, sewage-filled river, right next to the water towers. We'd passed the road when we'd first arrived, but there didn't seem to be anything there except overgrown wasteland. The man left us in front of a barbed-wire fence, where a half-built brick house was set back on a patch of dusty earth. Abigail clapped in the customary way, shouted to anyone at home, then finally ventured through the gate to knock on the door – but the place was completely deserted. An old man passing by told her that no one had lived there for at least a year.

After an entire day's searching we were still no closer to finding her. Finally admitting defeat, we returned, dejected, to our car.

"Wait," Dean suddenly exclaimed as we were about to drive off. "Over there – look! Isn't that her?"

He pointed to another small dwelling on the opposite side of the road, surrounded by a makeshift wooden fence, almost completely obscured by the scrub. Sure enough, just about visible in the dirt yard was the small, thin figure of a young girl. Silhouetted this time against the bright afternoon sun, not the glare of truckers' headlights, we immediately recognized her as that same girl in the lilac dress we had met just over a year ago. This time she was wearing a cream top painted with red roses, and blue denim shorts which clung awkwardly to her bony hips.

Incredibly, she recognized us too, beaming a broad smile as we walked up to her. "How did you find me here?" she asked as Dean and I gave her a hug. Before we could answer she bounded off around the back of the house to fetch her older brother and younger sister, shouting their names excitedly.

Leidiane was clearly the same childish, ingenuous girl we had met on the motorway that night. But her face had aged dramatically in the last year, almost as if she had an older woman's head on a child's body. Her hair, painted a DIY mousey blonde, was matted and scruffy, her teeth crooked and rotten, and her features jagged. She reminded me of many of the girls I used to work with on the streets of Belo Horizonte, whose young bodies had been wasted away by heavy drugs use, who no longer cared about appearance or personal hygiene.

Leidiane introduced us to her older sister, Vanessa, seventeen, a taller girl with a hardened look, yet who was just as thin as her sibling, and her chatty brother Lucas, eleven, who had clearly used the same hair dye as his sister to colour his tight curly locks. They all wanted to know why we'd spent the day searching for Leidiane.

I explained: "Dean is a singer. He wrote a song about you, Leidiane. He wants to know more about you, he wants to help you. Can we talk?"

Leidiane looked behind her. "My mum's here. She doesn't know what I do. Can we go somewhere else?"

Leidiane, her brother and sister, climbed in the back of the car and chatted excitedly as we drove to an ice cream parlour, close to Abigail's house. "I'm famous! I'm famous!" Leidiane sang as she listened to Dean's song. In the ice cream parlour, the three piled their plastic tubs high, and helped themselves to biscuits, cake, and fizzy drinks. Abigail said goodbye and went home. But as we began to talk to Leidiane about her life, she refused to admit that she sold her body on the motorway, or that she had ever touched a single rock of crack.

"I used to do 'programmes', but not any more," she said, fidgeting on her seat.

"That's not what we heard, Leidiane. They said you're there every night, behind Mineral Water," I said.

Leidiane screwed up her face in anger. "Who told you that? I bet I know who it was, those meddling b******s! I'm going to get them next time I see them!"

"We just want to help you. Remember what we said the last time we saw you, that you deserve so much more. If you want a better life, we could…"

But by now Leidiane was altered, incandescent with rage. "How dare they?! I'm going to kill them, you'll see!" she shouted, causing others sitting at nearby tables to watch us nervously.

This was a different girl from the vulnerable child we'd met on the side of the motorway, or the excited, singing girl in the back of our car. But I recognized the signs, too – those of a girl hopelessly addicted to crack. In the short time she spent with us she became increasingly erratic, unable to sit still and easily angered. Her brother and sister, too, were showing signs of withdrawal. By the time we decided to leave all three were asking us for money, and becoming aggressive when we said we couldn't give them any.

"You wrote a song about me, so you should give me money for it," Leidiane said as we drove them back home.

"We want to help you, but we won't give you money to buy drugs," I replied.

"I told you already, I don't use drugs! Just give me 10 reals so I can have some lunch," she replied, pulling nervously at the seat belt around her chest and kicking the door with her feet.

Perhaps expecting us to give in to her demands, Leidiane's sister turned on her: "Don't give her any money – she'll just buy crack with it. But me, I just want to eat. You're not going to let me go hungry, are you?"

"You're the one who'll smoke it, you *piranha*," Leidiane snarled back.

We arrived back at their house and Dean and I got out of the car to say goodbye. Vanessa ran straight inside without a word, followed by their brother. Leidiane turned around. "Go on," she said, sweetly this time. "Just 10 reals."

"I'm sorry," I told her.

"You're really not going to give me anything? Well, don't bother coming back." She swung around and walked off too, not towards home like the others, but in the opposite direction, towards the roar of cars and trucks hurtling along the motorway a few streets away.

Dean and I got back in the car and also made our way back to the BR-116, which would now take us further north as our journey began in earnest. After the elation of finally finding "Leilah" after so much searching, we now felt totally deflated. Dean in particular had pinned so much hope on finding the girl from his song, imagining she would reach out to us for help. Yet the reality wasn't as simple. Leidiane was just twelve – younger than we'd thought – yet she was already submerged in a world of crack addiction. All this young girl lived for was her next fix. She was physically incapable of contemplating a life without it. And she would do anything to get it, even if that meant being abused and assaulted in a truck driver's cabin.

As we drove out of Governador Valadares, once again passing that spot where we had first seen her, something else was tormenting Dean.

"We got here too late," he said, staring out the passenger window. "We left it a year, and we lost her."

We didn't know if Leidiane had turned to drugs to numb the pain of her nightly ordeal on the motorway, or if she had started selling her body to feed her habit, but the former seemed far more probable. A year earlier she was a different girl, she seemed more reachable, just a child unwillingly forced into a hellish existence to feed her poor family. Between then and now she had fallen headlong into the abyss, and, with no one to catch her, had hit rock bottom. She seemed tragically beyond saving. And all at the age of just twelve.

For that reason our second encounter with "Leilah" was far more heartbreaking than the first. It was perhaps also a wake-up call that the problem of child prostitution on this vast motorway was far more complex than we had thought. These girls were not just victims of circumstance, but slaves to so many other things, like drug addiction, and, as we would later discover, pimps, policemen, traffickers, an inept justice system, so many people with so many vested interests. It was certainly a reminder of the urgency of this tragedy, that in just a matter of months a precious young life could be destroyed.

But if we thought that losing a young girl to crack addiction was as bad as it could get, we were wrong. We were about to discover the worst that could happen.

*Chapter 5*

# Living Dead

The BR-116 stretched out before us for mile after mile, a dusty ribbon that coiled around hills, undulating with the contours of the land. We cut through lush green forests, neat coffee plantations, and straight corridors lined with bowing bamboo trees, but mostly wild *cerrado* plains, sun-scorched grasslands dotted with termite mounds and twisted, leafless trees. Every so often we would pass through a small town, where boys would accost us with bags of home-made cheese, sweetcorn toasted at the roadside, or vodka bottles filled with honey or home-made *cachaça* rum.

Night had fallen by the time we arrived in Padre Paraíso, a small town which seemed to appear out of nowhere at the end of a long, meandering climb around the hills. The place was poorly lit and eerie, its buildings all facing towards the motorway as they rose up the steep hillsides on either side. It seemed like an obscure, forgotten place, but I'd heard the name before, numerous times in fact, as I'd researched for this trip. I'd also come across the name of one of its residents, Sônia, who had been quoted in various newspaper and internet articles about children's issues in the region.

It wasn't difficult to find Sônia's house. She lived on a narrow, cobbled street running parallel to the BR-116, behind a petrol station and a row of scruffy shops and warehouses. She was a jolly, amiable woman who fussed over us, chatting and chortling as she ushered us into her large, immaculately furnished home and sat us down at a large oak dining table. A parakeet chirped in a cage and a wooden ceiling fan whirred above us as we talked.

We soon discovered that Sônia's jovial demeanour was covering up a very heavy heart. A devout Catholic, she'd spent her life responding to the need she found around her, helping where she could, even sometimes taking destitute young people into her home. Padre Paraíso, she explained, was the first town in the Jequitinhonha Valley, a name synonymous throughout Brazil with extreme poverty, where until very recently it was common for children to die from malnutrition.

"Every day a child would die," she remembered. "One day, five children from the same family passed away. It was terrible. So we decided to do something. We started a soup kitchen, we fed them, we helped their families. It worked, we managed to stop the children from dying."

The girls Sônia helped were now aged around twelve and thirteen. "But my heart still breaks for them," she said. "Oh yes, we saved their lives. But these days they're more dead than alive. I see them standing there at the side of the motorway, selling their bodies to the truck drivers. There's no life left in their eyes. I call them 'living dead'."

Thanks to the arrival of some social policies, like family benefits and food parcels, people in Padre Paraíso were no longer dying from malnutrition, she went on. Brazil's rapid development over the last decade had also started to trickle into the town, lifting some of its residents out of grinding poverty. But most families here were still desperately poor, and for hundreds of teenage girls the arrival of wealth had actually made matters worse. Before, everyone was poor, nobody could afford designer clothes, mobile phones, or fashionable beauty products, Sônia explained. Today, though, some had and some had not, and many of the town's poor girls had turned to prostitution to obtain the material things they wanted, which they thought they needed to be "somebody".

"I cared for them when they were tiny. I feel like they're my own daughters," said Sônia, her voice charged with emotion. "So imagine what it does to me when I hear that one of them has climbed into a truck and gone off up the motorway. Sometimes I never see them again. I can't take that."

Padre Paraíso was, Sônia explained, a supply town for child prostitution. There were so many young, pretty girls willing to sell their bodies, or take huge risks to escape the stigma of poverty, that they had become known as easy pickings for pimps and brothel owners. The fact that they were simple, naive country girls also made them ideal prey for human traffickers. They would travel for hundreds of miles to this inconspicuous little town nestled in the mountains to take back its young daughters, who would go off with them under the illusion that they would find the lives their mothers never had.

The most notorious, Sônia explained, was a woman who called herself Gaú. She came from a brothel in a place called the Cow's Head, somewhere hundreds of miles north in the vast, barren state of Bahia, and over the years she had left Padre Paraíso with dozens of young girls. Some had never returned. Others told of how they'd been held captive in dingy, windowless bedrooms, forced to have sex with strangers many times a night, and saddled with an ever-increasing debt they could never repay.

"Just last week I discovered that three sisters I know had agreed to go off with someone, who had told them they were going to work in the home of a rich family. When I heard that the place was called the Cow's Head, my heart nearly stopped. But it was too late – I didn't have time to warn them."

"How old are they?" I asked.

"Thirteen, fourteen, and sixteen."

Dean's eyes raced as I stopped the conversation to translate what Sônia had said.

What we were hearing was something more sinister than anything we had come across so far. Just the name of this brothel conjured up nightmarish, horror movie images, even before you knew the terrible things that were happening there. I later discovered that the name of the woman, Gaú, is an Indian word meaning "cow". It all seemed almost too hideous to be true.

"Fofa, she was one of the girls who managed to make it back," said Sônia, perhaps sensing my incredulity. "She's working at a restaurant now, just round the corner. Come on."

\* \* \*

Eat Well was a scruffy diner facing the motorway, its illuminated sign blackened by exhaust fumes. One man sat alone at one of the white plastic tables, hungrily shovelling rice and beans into his mouth, but otherwise the place was empty. The arrival of three more customers brought a young woman scurrying out of the kitchen, notepad and pen at the ready. As soon as she laid eyes on Sônia, though, she broke out a smile and strode over to give her a long hug.

Andréia – otherwise known as Fofa – was a cheerful, chatty 21-year-old woman with a sunny disposition. You certainly would never have guessed that she'd once had to endure the kind of horrors that Sônia had just been describing. She was one of those babies who owed their lives to Sônia and her friends, she told us, but like so many of the young girls, she had fallen into the world of prostitution at an early age. She stayed on her feet and leaned over us, putting both hands on the table as she spoke.

"I'm not ashamed of talking about it," she told us. "I sold my body when I was young, but that's normal here. I thank God that I'm out of it now, though. I lived to tell my story, but a lot of the others didn't."

Andréia was thirteen and had been working on the BR-116 in Padre Paraíso for nearly two years when she met Gaú, the woman from the Cow's Head.

"She was older, in her thirties, a *morena* (brunette), and seemed really kind. She'd come to the motorway at night and bring us presents, lipstick, perfume, that kind of thing. She came back night after night. One night she said she knew of a place where there were parties every night, with free drinks and lots of men with money, and asked if I wanted to go with her.

"So I went. We hitched a lift with a truck driver going north. I had to sleep with him to pay for the ride, but I was so young and stupid, even that didn't make me realize what was really happening.

"I'm not sure how long we travelled for, but it was a long time, at least a day and a night. It was dark when we got there. I looked out and saw a row of bars on the side of the motorway. Music was blasting out and there were men everywhere, truck drivers. Gaú took me by the arm and walked me over to one of the bars, which had naked women painted on the walls. The men all shouted and made obscene gestures as I walked past them. That's when I started getting scared.

"I was taken to a bedroom behind the bar. It was tiny, just enough room for a bed, and had no windows. They told me I owed them Gaú's fee for bringing me, and the rent of the room, and that I'd have to sleep with men to pay it off. They said I wouldn't leave that room until I did. I started shaking and crying, I was terrified. Then the men started coming. I'd lost count by the end of that night."

Andréia spent a month locked in that brothel bedroom, a living nightmare that seemed to never end. She was the youngest girl, offered to men who wanted to pay more for a *novinha* ("little girl"), but kept out of sight in case the authorities turned up. Finally, she managed to persuade a man to ring her family back in Padre Paraíso, who travelled up there, threatening to call the police if the brothel owners didn't let her go. They released her, probably preferring not to risk attracting unwanted attention; and besides, they knew there were many more girls like her where she'd come from.

"It was a terrifying experience," said Andréia. "It made me realize it wasn't worth it, that I needed to change my life. I didn't go back to the motorway after that. But there were more girls at the Cow's Head who were trapped like me. I don't know what happened to them."

It was already 11 p.m., so Dean and I said goodnight to Sônia and wandered along the edge of the motorway towards our lodgings for the night at the Three Brothers, a scruffy guesthouse overlooking a petrol station forecourt. Our minds were spinning, full of the images we had needed to mentally draw during the last few hours – this evil woman Gaú, the Cow's Head, those dark brothel bedrooms. What we had just been hearing, from a smiling, likeable young woman in the most ordinary of settings, was a story of human trafficking, pure and simple.

And, according to Sônia, it was still going on. Children still being snatched from the dark corners of this remote Brazilian town, still being transported for hundreds of miles up this same motorway, completely unaware of the terrifying fate which awaited them. I thought of those three young sisters Sônia had mentioned, who had left for the Cow's Head a few days ago. They had probably arrived by now, and were probably already lying, frightened and alone, in one of those windowless rooms. The very thought made me shudder.

"Matt, don't we need to find the Cow's Head? Did Fofa say where it is? Is it far away?" asked Dean.

I'd been thinking the same thing. "I'm not sure," I said. "She said the nearest town was called Santo Estévão, but I've never heard of it." It was in the direction we were headed, though, so we decided to try to find it.

At that moment the hunger pangs that had perhaps seemed irrelevant up until now began to gnaw, and we decided to find something to eat, walking up a cobbled hill to Padre Paraíso's main square. The place was surprisingly pleasant, bright and bustling. Plastic tables were scattered over Portuguese patterned cobblestone; around them families, groups of young people and couples laughed and chatted. It was hard to look around without remembering the horror stories we had just heard first hand. I wondered how many of these people, like Andréia, were carrying with them their own terrible experiences of exploitation, how many had also been prey to pimps and people traffickers.

We ordered a *caldo de feijão*, a traditional bean broth, and managed to find an empty table, facing a beautiful colonial church, painted pink, which towered atop a long stone staircase into the clear night sky.

We were halfway through our *caldo* and deep in conversation when a waitress approached our table awkwardly.

"Er, those girls over there," she said, pointing discreetly behind her with her thumb. "They said they're waiting for you." We peered over, past the brightly lit square to a dark side road. There were two young girls leaning on a wall in the shadows, waving us over. Dean and I did our best to ignore them, but by the time we had finished eating they were still there, still trying to catch our attention. We decided to wander over.

"Phew, I thought we'd be here all night!" exclaimed one of them, a thin girl in a short, body-hugging red dress. Her friend, on closer inspection, was actually a transvestite, although he would have fooled some less discerning observers.

"Erm, do we know you?" I asked.

"Don't think so. But we saw you walking around. You look like you're looking for a good time."

The girl, Carolina, was sixteen, as was her friend "Bruna". They hung around the square every night, they told us, although if business was bad they'd go down to the motorway, where they would always find an oil-soiled trucker willing to hand over 10 reals. They often did "programmes" together, Carolina said – many of the clients liked it. I told Carolina and Bruna we weren't looking for that kind of good time, and asked if they'd heard of the Cow's Head.

"That's that place where you can earn good money, right? Yeah, lots of girls have gone there. I thought about going there myself, but they said I was too old. Oh well, the fewer girls here, better for me," said Carolina.

We said goodbye and began walking back, past the still lively town square, then through dark, deserted streets towards our hotel in front of the motorway. Dean was expressing his amazement at how openly prostitution operated in the town. "I mean, look, just ten minutes sitting in the square, and we get approached by two girls."

I stopped in my tracks. "Dean, you do know that Bruna was a man, right?"

There was an awkward silence. "Er, yeah... of course... I mean, why would I have thought she was a girl? She, er, he, didn't look a bit like a girl."

It was a moment I didn't let him forget.

\* \* \*

The heat seemed intent on suffocating us as Dean and I arrived, covered in sweat, at the top of a steep red dirt hill. Squinting under a harsh mid-morning sun, we gazed upon a long row of identically built cottages, each painted a different bright colour under red clay roof tiles. They were *casas populares*, simple homes provided by the council for needy families. We were looking for No. 43, a green house behind a grey plastered wall, owned by a woman named Roxa.

It wasn't Roxa who came to open the metal gate, but her eldest daughter Natália, a shy, quiet girl who smiled at us but kept her eyes on the floor. We explained that Sônia had sent us to speak to her mum, and she led us over the dusty front yard into her home, which was cramped and dark, and where a thin, frail-looking woman sat forlornly on the arm of a sofa draped in red. She turned and looked at us, her eyes betraying a deep, overwhelming sadness.

"*Senhora* Roxa," I said, offering my hand. "We're sorry to intrude. We wanted to know more about your daughter, Natiele."

At that moment she gripped my hand tightly, bowed her head and began to sob, her whole body shaking. "God sent you here to comfort me," she whimpered. "This morning I asked him to help me, because I can't take the pain any more."

Sônia had already told us something of what was behind this woman's tears, and it was a tragedy that would have shattered any family. But she hadn't warned us just how broken this poor woman still was, how inconsolable after so many years. Dean sat down beside her on the arm of the sofa and put his arm around her as she talked, her frail, high-pitched voice sometimes turning into a desperate, inconsolable wail.

It was seven years ago when her fourteen-year-old daughter Natiele went missing from Padre Paraíso. Like most days, she had been selling bunches of chives on the streets to help provide some money for her mother.

"She was a good Christian girl. It was completely unlike her," Roxa assured us. "She helped me so much, she brought me money back so I could buy food. One night she didn't come home."

Roxa was beside herself with worry, imagining the worst, when one of Natiele's friends helped to put her mind at rest: she had gone to work in the home of a rich family, she told her, and would soon come back with her earnings, which would be many times more than the small amount she got from selling her chives. The place where she had found a job was called the Cow's Head, and the woman who took her there was Gaú.

It was four months later when Roxa's world came crashing down. Police arrived at her home with the devastating news that Natiele had been found dead, nearly a thousand miles away in the north-eastern state of Rio Grande do Norte. Her life had ended inside a trucker's cabin, where she had been brutally beaten over the head and shot through the chest. Natiele's death certificate documented those terrifying moments in chilling detail: "An extremely violent death," it read, "caused by cranial trauma, thoracic laceration, projectile from a firearm."

Nobody knows exactly what happened to Natiele after she left Padre Paraíso, if she had been forced into prostitution at the Cow's Head before leaving for a life working the motorways, or if she was also being held against her will inside that truck too, perhaps being transported to another place. Whatever nightmare she had been living ended at 3.30 p.m. on 9 August 2004, the moment her mother Roxa's living nightmare began.

"I was at home when they came," she said, gripping Dean's hand firmly. "It was pouring with rain. My brother came in first, then the police. I thought they were finally bringing my daughter home. I don't remember anything else. I collapsed. I was getting my daughter back, but in a coffin."

The shock was so great that Roxa's body shut down. For a year she didn't say a single word, and for the next two years she was paralysed on one side and was unable to walk. Even now, she was a fragile shadow of what she once had been, and claimed her eyes were too weak to let sunlight into her house. She hardly ever left her home, could only manage to walk a few yards, and spent most of her days in the dark, sitting on the arm of that old red sofa.

"They carried me to the place to recognize her," Roxa remembered. "They only showed me a tiny part of her face. That was the last time I saw her. I couldn't even make it to the funeral."

I asked her if she could show me a photo of Natiele. Tears once again welled up in Roxa's vacant eyes. "I burned all of them," she said. "I can't bear to see her. I would die if I ever saw her beautiful face again.

"She had lovely cascading curls. Her skin was pale and perfect. I can see her here today. She's a blessing, helping me around the house, smiling, taking me on walks. Oh, God, what am I going to do without her…"

Dean fought back tears as he held Roxa closer, her voice rising again to an agonized wail.

Dean asked what happened to the truck driver who had taken away this young life with such violence and brutality.

"He escaped, they never caught him," Roxa replied. "He's probably still driving up and down this cursed motorway. The same with the woman who seduced her. Sometimes I hear she's back in town, befriending other girls. It's not fair. I want to know who took my daughter's life. I want him to see what he did to that girl's mother and sisters."

As Roxa spoke, Natália busied herself around the house, putting rice to boil in the kitchen, brushing the floor. Her two sisters, thirteen-year-old Jaqueline and eleven-year-old Talita, stayed quietly in one of the bedrooms. As we got ready to leave I asked Natália what life was like for them since their sister's death.

She smiled sadly. "It was terrible for all of us when our sister died, but we're all just about all right now. But my mum isn't. She never goes out, she just closes the shutters and sits like a statue in there. We tell her to get herself well again, that she's got other daughters who need her, but nothing works."

It was the greatest tragedy we'd found inside that bright-green house: that those three young girls hadn't just lost their older sister, but their mother too. That home should have been full of life and laughter, but instead it was a place of sadness, where Natiele's sisters were virtual orphans, their mother just a vacuous shell, a motionless shadow in the darkness of her living room.

As we emerged back into the blinding sunlight, I too began to think of the man who did this. How many times,

I wondered, had young Natiele's murderer passed by on the motorway below them in the last eight years? And the evil woman Gaú, where was she now? How many more young lives had she had a hand in destroying?

But the BR-116 had robbed many more mothers of their young daughters in this small, insignificant town. According to Sônia, inside many of the tiny dwellings dotted around these steep red hills were others, hoping against hope that their girls were all right and that they would see them again. Others, like Roxa, were having to deal with the certainty that they wouldn't.

One of the most recent cases which shocked the people of Padre Paraíso was that of Ana Flávia, an eleven-year-old girl from the town who died in the cabin of a truck which crashed on the BR-116. A number of people who we'd spoken to over the last few days had mentioned her. A trucker had picked up her and another girl as he drove through Padre Paraíso late one night, an encounter which would end in tragedy an hour later in a wreck of mangled metal near Teófilo Otoni, a town fifty miles further south.

Sônia knew Ana Flávia – she had been in her class at the school where she taught – and she filled me in on the story:

"She was a beautiful, sweet girl," she remembered. "She started dropping out of class when she was just nine or ten. Older girls who were experienced on the road would take her out with them. They'd take trucks together and no doubt encouraged her to do the 'programmes'.

"From then on I didn't see her again, I just heard about where she'd been seen, how far away she'd travelled. I remember thinking it was just a matter of time before something terrible happened."

A year before she died, Ana Flávia was involved in another serious accident. She and another girl, Tatiane, fourteen, were with a truck driver travelling north, approaching the town of Cândido Sales, 100 miles north of Padre Paraíso in the state of Bahia. As they drove down a steep hill he lost control, crashed through a narrow bridge, and plunged into a ravine below. The driver died and the two girls were taken to hospital with serious head injuries.

"Ana Flávia was hurt the worst. She was in hospital for days and nearly didn't make it," Sônia remembered. "She ended up with a huge scar across that beautiful face of hers. But it didn't stop her from going to the motorway. On the contrary, it was almost as if she didn't care any more what happened to her."

It was on 24 May 2011 that Ana Flávia's young, messed-up life was finally extinguished. Speeding along the hard shoulder, undoubtedly distracted by the two girls in his cabin, the driver didn't see a broken-down lorry in the darkness. The impact crumpled the passenger side of the cabin, precisely where Ana Flávia was sitting. Entangled in the wreckage, she hung on to life for nearly an hour, according to rescue crews who tried to cut her free. She died before they could. Her friend, a fifteen-year-old called Aline, was taken to hospital and survived. The cowardly driver, however, was nowhere to be seen. He had fled, leaving two frightened girls trapped, one quickly losing her fight for life.

Everybody we asked knew where Ana Flávia's mum lived, halfway up a cobbled road rising up the opposite side of the valley. Her eight-year-old daughter let us in, taking us into another dark living room where, stretched out on a sofa, a woman with peroxide-blonde hair stirred underneath a thick blanket. Seeing us there, she sat upright, fixing her hair with her hands.

"Look, I work nights, so this time of the day is sacred for me. I don't appreciate being disturbed when I'm trying to sleep," she said sharply.

"We're really sorry, we didn't know. We can come back later," I said, stepping back towards the door.

"What do you want, anyway?"

I explained that we were hoping to tell others about the terrible things that were happening to young girls on the BR-116, and how sorry we were to hear about her daughter.

"Well, I'm sorry too but I don't want to talk about that. It's in the past, finished. I don't see any point in bringing it up again."

"I completely understand, no problem," I said. "Sorry to disturb you…"

"I mean, nothing I say is going to bring her back. What happened caused a lot of bad stuff, and no one seems to care how I'm coping. I regret ever becoming a mother – it causes too much pain and suffering. I'm sorry to disappoint you, but I just don't want to talk about all that."

We stayed there for half an hour, with Ana Flávia's mother insisting she didn't want to talk, but at the same time telling us everything. She was dealing with her grief differently to Roxa, facing up to it with anger rather than letting it steal away her strength, but it was clearly just as deep, just as raw, and just as debilitating. She, like Roxa, hardly ever left the four walls of her small rented brick house, except to go out to work. And although she wasn't physically weak like Roxa, she was just as beaten down, cynical, and life-weary, as if the tragedy had robbed her of any belief she might have had in the goodness of people.

Her eight-year-old daughter, like Roxa's daughters, was also being affected, missing out on a happy childhood. When I asked her if she missed her sister, she smiled sarcastically: "What, my older sis, the one who died and who I'll never see again? Er, yes, I think so."

Ana Flávia's mother continued to chastise us for being there, and yet continued to open up. Her night shift, it turned out, was working the motorways and petrol station forecourts. She would lock her daughter alone in her house until she returned, often as dawn was breaking.

"I'm not ashamed, I have to put food on the table," she told me. "Most single mothers in Padre Paraíso live off truck drivers' cash – I'm no different from anyone else. Even so, there are people trying to stick their noses in my business, reporting me for leaving a child alone. I don't have any friends here. I don't want anything to do with them, they just make your life a misery."

Finally, she took out a clearly cherished box from underneath her TV cabinet, which contained the only two photos they had of Ana Flávia. One showed her, aged four, beaming with excitement as she made sandcastles on the beach in her bathing costume; in the other she was eight, just a normal, happy girl, posing with her younger sister. Seeing the pretty young girl for the first time, I began to choke back tears. It just seemed so tragic, knowing the direction that her life would take just a few years from then – used and abused on a dark, pitiless motorway, dead in the wreck of the very place where her innocence had been stolen.

"She was a really good girl. She never wanted for anything," said Ana Flávia's mother. "Her head got messed up at school. She got involved with the wrong crowd, that's when she started taking truck rides here and there. I gave her so much good advice, I really did."

I asked her about the truck driver. "The police found out who he is, but that's all they did. They never caught him. They say the case is in the hands of the courts, but it's been more than a year now and nothing's happened. I doubt anything ever will. I'll stay here in this *inferno*, my heart breaking for my little girl, and he'll still be driving past on the motorway down there. I just want him to pay for what he did. That's what makes me most angry – the injustice of it all."

Injustice. It was a theme Dean and I would come across time and again during the next thousand miles north. These girls were apparently too insignificant, too unimportant, for Brazil's selective justice system to bother standing up for them. They could be trafficked, imprisoned, left for dead or even murdered, and society barely noticed, let alone going after their abusers.

As we walked back down the hill, our calf muscles straining with the steep incline, Dean and I were thinking about the one who sees every act of injustice, no matter how inconsequential its victims. As Christians we believed in a God whose very nature is justice, who comforts the broken and defends the rights of the poor; it was this conviction which had brought us here. Right now though, we could entirely understand why Ana Flávia's family may not believe in this God of justice.

We later found out there were thirty-five churches in Padre Paraíso, common in a country which has the second-largest evangelical population in the world; one was called "The Church of The Revival" and they were busy raising money to build a shiny new temple. Meanwhile, the town's young girls were being snatched from the streets, and families were left lost and bereft, with neither comfort nor justice. Ana Flávia's mum would be right to ask where God was in the midst of so many Christians.

## Chapter 6
# Precious Stones

So dense was the darkness, we could barely see our hands in front of our faces. Tall, thick-set eucalyptus trees towered above us on both sides, shutting out even the moonlight. We shuffled forward warily on loose stones, unsure of where we were treading. Only when a truck screeched around the tight bend would our path be illuminated for a few brief seconds.

It was 10 p.m. and we were walking along the shoulder of the BR-116 outside Padre Paraíso. It was difficult these days, Sônia had explained, to encounter an underage girl selling her body back in town, where the motorway was bathed in the soft light of shop signs and sulphur street lamps. Truck drivers were unlikely to risk picking up a child where there was a chance they could be seen. So the younger girls would plunge into the pitch black, walking further up the motorway to the north or south of town, where there are no lights, buildings or prying eyes, and where the darkness covers everything.

We had negotiated the curve and were on a straight stretch. Sure enough, as the lights of the next truck rose up on the horizon, there was the silhouette of a girl, gesturing for a ride. The driver sounded his horn, but didn't stop. We made use of the light to walk more briskly towards her.

The young girl didn't flinch as we approached, she just folded her arms, cocked her head to one side and stared towards us. She was wearing denim shorts and high heels, and was made up like a doll, with painted purple eyelids and bright-red blush on her cheekbones. I said hello and offered her my hand, which she held for a lingering few seconds, pouting her lips like an experienced woman of the night.

Look past the bravado, though, and you could still find a vulnerable child in this young girl's pretty brown eyes. Her name was Tatiane and she was fifteen, she told us. I immediately recognized the name: Ana Flávia's friend, who had been with her in a trucker's cabin when she had suffered the first accident. I asked if she was that same Tatiane.

"Oh, please, don't remind me! The day she died was the worst day of my life. I was so upset, I just cried non stop. I didn't sleep at night for weeks," she said.

"She must have been a good friend," I suggested.

"The best. We did everything together. Did you know she sent a message to me while she was dying? She recorded it on her phone and made one of the firemen promise to get it to me. I nearly had a heart attack when I watched it. She told me to stop going to the motorway, to get out of this life while I still could. She said she didn't want me to end up dead too. She was thinking of me right up to the moment she passed on."

"So what on earth are you doing here?"

"I stopped for a while. What else am I supposed to do? I like wearing nice clothes and going to parties. I'm high maintenance."

Another HGV stormed by, blasting its horn lewdly. Tatiane turned around and stuck up her middle finger defiantly.

Tatiane, it turned out, was another of the girls Sônia had rescued from almost certain death as a baby. She was already in an advanced state of malnutrition when, aged just eighteen months, her mother abandoned her on the street and ran away from Padre Paraíso, probably believing her daughter wouldn't last another night. She was taken in by a neighbour who, with Sônia's help, nursed her back to strength. The mention of Sônia's name caused Tatiane's eyes to light up and some of her hardness to melt away.

But before she had even reached puberty, at the age most other girls are playing with dolls and dressing up, Tatiane was already strutting along the side of the BR-116, selling her underdeveloped body to truck drivers. Before long, its lonely dark shoulders and blinding headlights had become everything she knew.

Tatiane said she charged 50 reals, although she admitted on most nights she'd accept half that, or even just the ride if she was getting a lift to another town.

I asked her about the accident she suffered with Ana Flávia.

"We used to travel all over the place together," she said. "We'd been standing just here when we got picked up. The guy was on his way north into Bahia. We didn't know where we'd end up. It was really late at night when I swapped with Ana Flávia. She went to the front with him and I went to the back. That's the last thing I remember. I stayed in hospital for four days. They said I was really lucky, look…"

She showed us a scar in the back of her head where she had been flung forwards in the impact and cracked her skull. "Ana Flávia was hurt even worse," she said. "All her teeth got smashed in and one side of her face was all messed up. The driver didn't stand a chance, he was crushed to death."

"And it still didn't make you stop?"

"We should have. If we had, Ana Flávia would still be alive today. But what else could we do? Our families couldn't buy us the stuff we wanted."

I asked Tatiane if anything could persuade her to leave the life of prostitution, and she shrugged her shoulders.

"My mum – the one who adopted me – used to try to stop me, but she doesn't say anything any more. She knows it won't work. She'd tell me I had to stay at home helping her around the house. But look at these hands – do you think they were made for washing dishes or scrubbing floors? No, I want to enjoy myself, I want to be able to wear nice clothes and have a good time. You see these shoes – they cost 300 reals. I'm not like these sad women who stay indoors getting old and ugly."

The delusion was staggering and incredibly sad. This girl was standing alone in the dust and darkness, being taunted by passing truck drivers, occasionally picked up for the most dirty and degrading of encounters, yet believing the money she was earning made her the envy of every woman in town. Just as Sônia had said, the young girls of Padre Paraíso were throwing their lives away for the most transient of things, swapping their most precious possession for status symbols like designer clothes and mobile phones, somehow believing they were living the life others could only dream of. If only they knew just how precious they were, how much they were really worth, how fulfilled and meaningful their lives could really be.

"You'll get old too one day, you know," I said, as we said goodbye. "Have you thought about what you'll do then?"

"Oh, that's a long way off yet," she replied, spinning round to face the oncoming traffic again as we wandered back towards the lights of town.

\* \* \*

Dean and I woke up early, grabbed a strong coffee and a piece of corn cake from the *pousada*'s sparse breakfast table and headed straight for the car. It was time to continue our journey north, and our next destination was Medina again, the place whose dark secrets had persuaded us to travel this vast highway, just over a year earlier. We were soon out of town and winding around that sharp curve before the stretch of straight road where we'd met Tatiane last night.

We'd expected to find nothing in the daylight but memories, and certainly not the sight that we now beheld.

Stretching out in the distance were dozens of metal stalls with yellow canvas roofs, each packed with brightly coloured stones which glistened in the morning sun. We pulled up at one to have a look. There were round geodes – hollow rocks cut in half, grey and mundane on the outside but packed with purple crystal formations on the inside; smooth, shiny gemstones of various sizes, intense blue aquamarines, green tourmalines, and orange imperial topaz. Some had been made into ornaments, like turtles and swans, or multicoloured wind-chimes which hung from the roof, gently jangling in the breeze.

I asked the stall owner where the stones had been mined.

"From right under your feet," he replied. "You're in the capital of precious stones, you know. You might not think there's anything that special around here, but deep down there, there exist some of the most beautiful, most valuable things you'll ever find in Brazil."

For ten miles underneath the stretch of motorway we were standing on, he told us, was the highest concentration of aquamarine in the world. Men were working down there all the time, risking their lives crawling through narrow tunnels dug into the hills, hoping to glimpse the crystals glistening in the darkness. Everyone dreamed of finding the next "big one", like the Dom Pedro Aquamarine, a near-flawless crystal weighing 10,395 carats discovered in 1993, or the Papamel Aquamarine, the largest aquamarine ever seen, found in 1910 and weighing a massive 552,500 carats.

Dean was interested in a box containing four tiny tourmaline gemstones each cut into tear shapes. Tourmaline happened to be the name of the area in Governador Valadares where we had first met Leilah by the side of the road. A precious stone with the same name, shaped like a tear, seemed like a poignant way of remembering her. He asked how much it would cost.

"I'll do you a deal – 50 reals for all four. There, you've got a bargain," said the stall owner.

Dean and I looked at each other. Fifty reals was the same price Tatiane sold herself for, and twice what little Leilah thought she was worth. Yet when it came to a handful of shiny stones dug from the earth, we were getting a bargain at twice the price. Both the stones and the girls were found in the darkness and dirt, both were sold on the side of the same stretch of road, yet one was treasured and precious, the other discarded and worthless. If only people placed as much value on those true precious stones, as on beautiful girls like Leilah and Tatiane, we thought. If only people here plucked them from the darkness with the same fervour, polished and treasured them with the same love and dedication.

Dean clutched his gemstones as we drove off. Our time in Padre Paraíso had revealed more hurt and heartache than we could have imagined. It was with a sense of trepidation that we made the two-hour journey north to Medina, where we already knew something of the stories we would encounter there. We had no idea, though, that the next few days would change our lives forever.

## Chapter 7
# Predators

Ith wasn't easy to reach twelve-year-old Lilian's house. We tried it a number of times, starting from the motorway, where vultures circled in slow spirals above a dusty slaughterhouse. From there, you take a dirt side road before turning left into a maze of narrow cobbled streets, right, second left, right, right... Every street looked identical and each time we ended up getting hopelessly lost.

Rita, of course, knew the way, but was sitting silently in the passenger seat, deliberately saying nothing. I wanted to see if I could get there on my own after she told us something unbelievably shocking: that, from when Lilian was just ten, truck drivers on their long journey north or south would leave the BR-116 and park their huge, forty-tonne vehicles outside her house, abusing her inside their cabins – and with the blessing of her mother.

"They knew the way by heart," Rita explained. "So whenever they passed by Medina they would drive their trucks right in and park up yards away from her home. Lilian's mother would just send her off, rub her hands together, and wait for her to come back with the money."

What Rita was describing was almost too disgusting for words. These were no chance encounters with some young temptress, dolled up and offering herself at the side of the road. Men who wanted to abuse Lilian needed to deliberately go looking for her, leave the motorway and negotiate the narrow streets and tight corners of one of Medina's poorest districts, where toddlers played in the dusty roads until late and neighbours sat chatting on doorsteps. They probably had to ask them for directions the first time, perhaps after hearing the child's name in the drunken bragging of another of her "clients". Then they had to have the nerve to park up, knock on the girl's door, sound their horn, or whatever was the agreed signal, before the deal was done and the trembling ten-year-old was sent out.

Dean was disgusted. "It's amazing – that the men here sit by as their girls are abused and nobody does anything about it. If this was happening in my hometown and the police weren't taking care of business – there'd be a posse of country boys banging on that trucker's door. It would be over."

"That's the biggest tragedy. Most people here don't think there's anything remotely wrong with it," explained Rita. "We never caught anyone because no one ever reported it. A girl in the family is an opportunity to make money, that's what they think."

The town, the first before the state border with Bahia, was a popular stop for truck drivers looking for a cheap liaison with an underage girl, Rita went on. Some who regularly passed through Medina already knew where to go, who to call, which of the drab, identical houses was actually a brothel, or even where the girls themselves lived. Others would just drive into the town square and try their luck, knowing that sooner or later they would find a child waiting in the shadows.

We'd only been back in Medina for a few hours and we were already reeling at the sheer scale of this tragedy. Being born a girl here seemed like a curse. What hope could these girls have when their own families colluded in robbing them of their hopes and dreams, denying them their right to be a child?

We eventually did reach Lilian's home, this time under Rita's guidance. Rita spotted her straight away, not near her house, a small brick building on the corner of a steep hill, but in a crowded bar blasting out *forró* music on the opposite side of the road. We watched as the small girl danced provocatively among a group of rowdy, drinking men, a glowing cigarette between her fingers.

Rita called her over and she skipped down the hill towards us. She had a child's face and a pretty, shy smile. Rita asked where her mum was.

"Oh, she found a boyfriend and went off with him. They say she's getting beaten up by him now. I'm living over there with my grandmother now."

Her "grandmother", Rita quickly discovered, wasn't any relation at all, but an older neighbour who had taken her in. It was she who was sending Lilian to the bar, probably expecting her to repay her "kindness" by seducing drinkers and bringing the money home. Lilian just smiled when I asked how a mother could just abandon her daughter when a new man arrived on the scene. She had no idea what it was to be loved by anyone. Being used, then discarded, was all she had ever known.

Lilian would disappear for days, sometimes weeks at a time, Rita explained, running off with other girls her age, ending up in towns or roadside bars hundreds of miles up or down the motorway. Or more often she would be taken off by a relative or neighbour and used, as always, as a bargaining tool; whether it was a ride to another town, a night's lodgings, or just a plate of food, they knew they could get everything with a pretty twelve-year-old to offer in exchange. Lilian had recently discovered she was pregnant, but a month ago she lost the baby in what Rita suspected was a dangerous back-street abortion – possibly forced on her by the many who had vested interests in this young girl.

"No, I fell off a motorbike and the baby died, that's what happened," Lilian insisted.

Rita lived in fear of one day receiving the worst possible news about Lilian. And that day had nearly come almost a month ago, when, one night in another bar, she was stabbed in the back during a fight. Lilian showed us the scar just below her neck.

"I was terrified, I thought I was going to die," she said. "I passed out and woke up in hospital. The doctor said if it had been just half an inch either way, I wouldn't have woken up at all."

Lilian nodded as Rita told her off for giving her such a scare, and told her that a bar wasn't a place for a child like her, and that she didn't want to catch her there again. We told her how special she was, how she could turn her life around and be anything she wanted to be, but deep inside I knew the odds were almost impossibly stacked against her. Buffeted from place to place, lacking any positive reference in her life, and with nowhere in this town where she could go to escape this daily cycle of abuse and exploitation, how could this young girl be expected to believe in herself and go after her dreams? That is, if she still had any. I asked her, and we were surprised at her response.

"I want to be a public prosecutor," she said. "Look." She turned round, and for the first time we noticed what was written on the back of her one-shoulder black top, the words of a Latin proverb: "Let justice be done, though the world perish." Perhaps we shouldn't have been surprised at all that this silent victim of injustice wanted to speak up for others who were powerless and forgotten. It was a sign that there was still hope, that Lilian's dreams hadn't yet been completely buried.

We were walking across the road to the car when Rita noticed a group of children playing in the dusty front yard of the house opposite. Among them were two sisters, Lilian's cousins, who she had been accompanying as part of her work at the children's council. As we talked to them the younger sister, aged ten, chatted and leapt between rocks, throwing stones at tin cans and writing with her finger in the red earth. The eldest, however, said nothing. Poliana, a small, skinny twelve-year-old, just sat motionless, her eyes fixed on the ground, gnawing on the nails of both her thumbs. She looked fragile and deeply traumatized.

"Hey, Poliana, what's wrong? What happened to you? This isn't like you," asked Rita, resting a hand on her shoulder. Still, the young girl didn't even glance towards her. Yards away, her mother, her sagging flesh covered in tattoos, stood chatting with another woman, eyeing us suspiciously.

As we talked with the other children, as well as Poliana's mother, the look in Rita's eyes turned from concern to dismay to outright horror. Poliana, we discovered, had returned yesterday from a place called Veredinha, where her aunt had taken her and her sister. Veredinha was a small village on the margins of the BR-116 around fifty miles north of Medina, but I had heard of it and understood why Rita was so alarmed – the place was notorious for its high incidence of child prostitution. The remote village, near the border with Bahia, was little more than a huge truck stop, with row after row of bars and brothels, and clients willing to pay for sex with a child, and knowing they could do so in impunity.

Poliana did eventually manage a smile, but the disturbed, frightened look in her eyes never went away. As we drove away Rita filled us in on her story.

"She's one of five sisters, aged between eight and thirteen. A few months ago the oldest girl came looking for me, begging me to take her and her sisters away from there. She said her mum's boyfriend was violent, that he'd come home drunk and beat them. She said she'd often take her sisters to the outside toilet to hide from him, and they'd sleep there all night.

"Their mother is the sister of Lilian's mother, and she was cast from the same mould. I knew it was just a matter of time before they were being initiated into prostitution, just like Lilian was. But I couldn't find anywhere for them to go. There are no children's homes in Medina and even the ones further away don't have any places."

Rita scrubbed a hand across her face. "The last time I saw Poliana she was so playful and chatty. Something terrible's happened to her. I should have tried to do more to get them out of there. I was too late… again."

I remember how, a year ago when we'd first met Rita, she'd described how the girls of Medina were being lost like a "handful of earth" falling through her fingers. Now we were beginning to see what she meant. I asked her about the girls we visited when we were last in Medina.

"Lost too, all of them," she replied.

"What do you mean?"

Viviane, the younger of the two sisters from the house in front of the motorway, had disappeared, she explained. Her sister last saw her getting into a truck, in broad daylight, telling her she'd be back in a week – that was three months ago. The young girl, now thirteen, still hadn't returned home, and no one knew where she was, or if she was even still alive.

The second house we'd visited was that of Letícia, now thirteen, whose father had been sick with worry, desperate to stop his young daughter's dangerous liaisons on the motorway. But in the twelve months since we met her

Letícia's life had gone into free-fall. She would go missing for weeks at a time, lost in a shadowy underworld of drugs, danger, and sex-crazed men. Rumours were also swirling that she had AIDS.

Then there was Mariana, the thirteen-year-old whose story had made such an impression on Dean and me a year ago. Since then we had made several attempts to take her away from the mother and grandmother who had forced her into a life of prostitution. Each time they had resisted, sometimes with veiled threats, and despite overwhelming evidence that they were using her to make money, Medina's judge had inexplicably refused to intervene.

Again, the news was as bad as it could be. Now just turned fifteen and seven months pregnant, she too was missing. Rita visited her family a few days earlier, and they told her they hadn't seen her for nearly three weeks, although they hadn't bothered to report it. Mariana had gone off with an older girl, and was believed to be in one of countless roadside brothels along the motorway north of Medina.

Rita's words came as a huge blow. Last year we'd left Mariana's house feeling that, given an opportunity, there was hope for this young girl who gushed over Justin Bieber and drew flowers and love-hearts in her notebooks. But right now all that hope had vanished, and we were left feeling, like Rita, that we could have done more, that we should have acted more quickly, that it was now too late to save her.

"Wait, turn in here," said Rita abruptly as we passed the entrance to a cobbled road lined with terraced cottages which seemed familiar. "That's Armando's house – you remember, Letícia's dad? Let's see if he's at home."

Armando wasn't at home – his son, Letícia's younger brother, appeared at the window, but asked us to wait as he called his father where he was working. Minutes later,

Armando came running down the road, panting heavily and with a look of alarm on his face.

"It's about Letícia, isn't it? Have you found her? What's happened to her?"

"No, no," said Rita calmly. "We just wanted to see how you were."

Armando caught his breath and placed his hand across his chest. "Thank God," he said. "I had a dream last night that she was dead. I thought you'd come to tell me."

Armando was the same tormented father, torn apart by his love for his wayward daughter. He'd learned to sleep at night, though, to let go of her a little, for the sake of his health, his son, and his elderly mother. Even so, every time his telephone rang his heart would pound out of his chest, he told us. Whenever he got word of where Letícia might be, he would drop everything to go and fetch her, even if that meant travelling for a hundred miles down the motorway. He was sure, though, that one day that trip would be to collect his daughter's dead body.

"It's inevitable. She's playing with death, every time she takes that motorway. I can't bear to think where she is now, what someone out there's doing to her."

I asked if he had any idea where Letícia was. "The last I heard, she was in a brothel in Ponto dos Volantes, just north of Padre Paraíso. They say it looks just like a normal house from the outside, that only the men who go there know it's where the young girls are. If I knew where it was I'd be there today to bring her home.

"I just want my daughter back, if that's still possible. She needs help. I just wish there could be somewhere she could go, someone to help her find herself again. Here in Medina no one wants to know about girls like her, they just think she's a nuisance. But I know her – she's caring, she's intelligent, she's got everything going for her. If only she knew that for herself."

\* \* \*

The crooning tunes of *sertaneja* music blared out of burger bars, mixing with the loud chatter of people eating and drinking as Dean and I threaded our way through the red plastic tables scattered around Medina's main square. We found an empty table and called over the waiter. Every so often a car packed with loudspeakers would coast by, blasting us for a few seconds with a different rhythm, pounding funk or hurried "*arrasta-pé*" *forró* music.

Dean and I didn't say much as we waited for our Cheese Everything burgers. Our minds were so full, our hearts so heavy, that the idle banter we normally enjoyed on nights like this just didn't seem appropriate. The terrible things we had seen and heard, the girls we had met, the feeling of anger yet powerlessness – it was all beginning to overwhelm us. For the next half an hour we exchanged some words, gazed up at the cloudless night sky, watched as cars and trucks coasted by around us, observed others enjoying a rowdy night out, shouting and laughing…

Then it suddenly dawned on me what was happening.

"Dean, that truck over there… what's he doing?"

We watched as the dirt-splattered dumper truck crawled around the square, stopping sporadically, then moving on again. After one lap it passed us again, then slowly drove around another time, then again, then again, before finally turning off into a dark side street and disappearing. Then there came another, an HGV which seemed almost too big to negotiate the road lined with parked cars. Again, it circled the square a number of times, hissing its air brakes, sometimes staying stationary for a few minutes. At one point there were three trucks moving slowly, sinisterly, around the square. They spent the most time at the furthest end, where there were few people and no street lights and where, Rita had told us, girls selling their bodies waited in the shadows for clients.

I remembered what Rita had said, that truck drivers would leave the motorway at Medina, try their luck in the town's busy nightspots, where they knew they would find young girls who could be bought for a price. And there they were, prowling the streets, circling the square like the vultures we'd seen earlier in the day spiralling over that ramshackle roadside slaughterhouse.

Suddenly it was all too much to bear. I couldn't stop the tears from welling up and streaming down my face. I saw Dean from the corner of my eye. Tears silently streaked from the shadow of his baseball cap, pulled low and over his eyes. After a long silence Dean whispered, "I only wish we could have reached Leilah."

People sitting nearby looked over and talked among themselves. Our waiter approached cautiously, unsure of what to say. I smiled and waved him away, then dissolved into tears again.

Dean and I cried silently on that packed square for nearly an hour. Every so often we would stop, but the images would quickly come flooding back: Leilah, sucked to the bone by addiction; Ana Flávia, that treasured photo of her beaming a smile as she made sandcastles with her sister; the inconsolable, crouched-up Poliana, having to come to terms with a violent and humiliating future; Armando, his life falling apart because his daughter just needed to know how special she was. What we really wanted to do was stand up and shout aloud to those chatting, laughing locals, demand to know how they could go on as normal, in the face of so much injustice, as fathers wept, as precious lives were being torn apart. And all the time the trucks kept circling.

"Matt," said Dean finally, "it doesn't seem right to just leave here and move on to the next place… we need to try and do something."

I agreed. The situation seemed just too urgent. These girls needed a way out. If we left it until later it might be too late for them.

Dean and I would look back on that night as a decisive moment in the most important journey of our lives. Wiping the tears from our eyes, we wondered if maybe there was a way to rescue the lost girls of the BR-116, and if there was, maybe it should begin in Medina. Maybe we could open a house, similar to the day centre in Belo Horizonte which, fifteen years earlier, had been so successful in changing the lives of that city's lost girls. It could have the same name – Meninadança – and, just like then, it would use the allure of dance to reach out to them, raise their self-esteem, and give them the strength to change. It would be a place where they would know they were safe, where there were people they could talk to, who cared for them, who would do everything they could to lead them back from the abyss. It would be a place where God's love would shine, where girls who had only known hurt and loneliness would find hope, healing, and justice.

*Chapter 8*
# Mariana

The following morning Dean and I talked with Rita about our plans to relaunch Meninadança in Medina, and as she listened relief – and a broad smile – spread across her face. It was everything she had longed to do for years, she told us. The idea of using dance and other girl-specific therapies was exactly how she had imagined reaching out to them, but without any support her dreams had remained just dreams, which she had grown tired of nurturing.

We spent the next few hours talking excitedly about what we could do, and allowing ourselves to imagine where it could lead. A network of dance centres, in towns along the BR-116, reaching out to girls trapped in child prostitution, showing them they were not alone and giving them hope; and safe houses, where girls who didn't have a family, or whose family were part of the problem, could go to live and learn to be children again. We knew that there was much to do, that there would be many hurdles to overcome and that it might take years before we got even close to where we wanted to be, but it has remained our ultimate goal.

Dean and I were due to leave Medina to continue our journey north, but Rita agreed to start looking for a property or piece of land where we could begin our work and for other people who could work with her.

Later that day, we heard news that increased our sense of urgency. Rita had gone back to speak again to Poliana and Lilian, but found neither of them. A neighbour told her that both had been taken away. Poliana's mother, perhaps nervous after we turned up asking questions yesterday, had whisked her and her two younger sisters off to a place by the motorway close to Governador Valadares, again notorious for prostitution, where she was almost certainly using them to earn money. And Lilian's aunt had gone off with her too – a friend said she needed to make a journey to a town even further away but didn't have any money for her travel or accommodation; she had taken Lilian with her "to make things easier".

\*\*\*

"Matt, I've just found out where Mariana is. She's staying in a brothel on the side of the 116. It's about halfway between here and the next town, Pedra Azul."

It was 9 p.m. and Dean and I were preparing for what was going to be our last night in Medina. We planned to continue our journey north, over the border into Bahia, where we knew there were other stories to be told, and where, somewhere at the Cow's Head, three of Padre Paraíso's young daughters were probably being held captive. We had arranged with Rita and her husband Max to meet for a farewell pizza at the only restaurant in town, but Rita had called in to reception before we had even got ready to go out.

"How did you find where she was?" I asked.

"I just spoke to one of her friends. She went with another girl called Fernanda, who's just twelve. Can you believe it was that girl's mother who took them there?"

By now nothing was surprising us, although it didn't make what she was saying any less shocking. I asked how long it would take to get there. "About half an hour. I'll see you in five, OK?"

We were soon driving through the gloomy blackness, occasionally dazzled by a truck's glaring headlights, as we followed the BR-116's twists and turns around the remote hills north of Medina. Meanwhile, Rita, sitting in the back, told us what she knew about the brothel we were heading to.

"It's hidden, most people wouldn't even notice it," she said. "But truck drivers far and wide know where it is, and that they can buy a young girl there. Last year we did a raid there with the police, and found four girls, between twelve and fourteen. They closed the place down, but it reopened a few months later as if nothing had happened... Here it is, quick, turn in now."

We pulled in to what at first seemed nothing more than a dusty stopping place next to the road. Just as Rita had said, no one but those in the know would have given it a moment's notice – by the time you'd caught sight of the dimly lit bar, set back in the trees, you would have already hurtled past. But there were already two huge cargo trucks parked in the narrow forest clearing. Peering towards the small brick building, illuminated from the inside, we could see the silhouettes of a billiard table, beer bottles on tables, a number of men, and a woman holding a baby in her arms.

"I don't think I should go in there," said Rita. "They'd remember me from the raid. I'll stay in the car – they'll think it's just you two."

Dean and I tried to hide our nerves as we walked over the pebbly ground towards the bar, where the barking of drunk men mixed with the decadent rhythms of *forró* music blasting out. Heads turned as we approached. The idea was to sit down at one of the tables, ask for a beer, and make some discreet enquiries in the hope of coming across Mariana. However, we found her as soon as we stepped inside – dancing provocatively in front of a scruffy, unshaven man who held a billiard cue in one hand, a bottle of Brahma beer in the other. I'll never forget those few seconds before Mariana looked up and realized who we were. She was the same doe-eyed young girl we'd met a year ago in her home. But here, amid the cigarette smoke, the smell of *cachaça* rum and the clinking of bottles, she was going through the motions, doing what she had been taught. The man cackled excitedly, licking his lips as he held her hips, moving his hairy bare belly closer to hers, unbothered about the baby bulge which showed she was seven months pregnant.

I pointed at her jokingly and laughed to try to break the awkwardness. "Found you! I bet you never thought you'd see us again… Come outside, we need to talk."

Mariana immediately came over to us, leaving the man mumbling foul-mouthed protests as he took another swig of beer. The three of us walked back to the motorway's edge and sat down on a slab of concrete over an underground cistern. It was so dark we could hardly make out our hands in front of our faces. As we talked, the only moments we could see each other were when a truck roared by, lighting us up for a few seconds. Almost without fail, the truckers would blast their horns as they rumbled by, seeing the young girl sitting on the roadside, clutching her bare legs with her hands.

"What are you doing here?" I asked her. "This isn't a place for someone like you. I know it isn't the life that you want."

Mariana sighed. "My mum never cared about me. She was just interested in using me to buy her *cachaça*. So I ran away. At least now I can keep the money for myself."

"So is this it? When we talked last year you said you wanted to change your life. And now you've got to think about your baby too. What happened to all those dreams?"

"What am I supposed to do?" she whispered.

"Leave here and come back with us," I said. "Look, we never forgot you – that's how much you mean to us. Why not make a decision today, to leave all this behind and start a new life away from here?"

Mariana fell silent, her eyes glazed as she stared upwards at the stars perforating a cloudless sky. A man in denim shorts and a string vest stumbled out of the bar, urinated on the front wheel of his truck, then climbed inside and drove off. Mariana continued to gaze upwards.

"It's your grandmother, isn't it?" I asked. She nodded and wiped a tear from her face. Even though her grandmother had been the cause of her problems, the one who had made her believe prostitution was an option, Mariana still loved her dearly. And she knew that she wasn't strong enough to stand up to her and tell her she wanted to leave.

At that point we began to become aware of movement in the shadows around us, footsteps in the undergrowth. Dean began to pray under his breath as he caught sight of the darting silhouettes of men, circling us. Suddenly the place felt extremely dangerous and, although we were still persuading Mariana to leave, our hearts were beating furiously. Inside the car, Rita was also alarmed. With our blacked-out windows, no one had realized she was in there, or that she had watched two young men fetch revolvers from behind the bar and slowly come crouching, in our direction.

"Look, let's get you out of here," I told Mariana finally. "It will be easier for you to make a decision back in Medina. What do you think?"

Mariana nodded and we helped her up. Back in the car, Rita told us to get out of there quickly. I tore backwards and, glancing left and right, pulled out onto the motorway, spraying dust and loose stones behind us. We would never know what those men had planned for us, or how close we had come to losing our lives on that dark, remote patch of red earth. But we left there feeling even more acutely the lawless, violent world in which these girls exist, where men kill in cold blood and young girls disappear without a trace.

"Where should we take her?" I asked Rita as I saw the lights of Medina approaching. I assumed there would be some safe place where she could stay until the morning.

"We have to take her back home," she replied.

I looked round at her, shocked. "But that's where she ran away from. Once she's back there, her grandmother will never let her come away with us. It will be impossible."

"It's the law," Rita replied. "We have to deliver the child back to her family, until the judge makes a decision."

We drove through town and up the steep hill to Mariana's home, using the final few minutes to persuade her to come to the children's council in the morning. We would then talk to the prosecutor again, and try one more time to convince her to remove Mariana from her family, and let us take her away to somewhere safe where she could rebuild her life. We told Mariana she would need to be strong, make up her mind, and not listen to her mother and grandmother.

As we pulled up in front of Mariana's house, her mother was sitting on the mound of earth outside, puffing on a rolled-up cigarette, almost exactly as she'd been when we first met her. Seeing her daughter inside our car, she began to scream and swear.

"What did you bring this ****ing whore back for? She's worth nothing. All she does is cause me trouble. What an ungrateful b****, after everything I've done for her. You should have left her where you found her."

Tears began to pour down Mariana's face as she heard her mother berating and belittling her. It was so hard to just hand her over, not knowing what those cruel words would do to her fragile resolve, or what would happen in that dirt-strewn hovel before sunrise. As we drove back to our hotel, Dean and I were emotionally shattered by the whole thing. How could we expect such a broken, battered young girl to have the willpower to get up in the morning, defy the threats and emotional blackmail of her family, and decide to leave behind the only life she had ever known – all on her own?

We said goodnight and shut our bedroom doors behind us. I learned some time later that Dean had sat on his bed that night and sobbed uncontrollably as the injustice and madness of it all finally hit him. Alone in my room, I paced round and round, tears streaming down my face also. The abuse and exploitation being suffered by these precious children was too much to bear. And now the fragile life of Mariana hung in a skewed balance – the life of one beautiful girl – one girl who represented the plight of thousands. What could matter more in this world than trying to save them?

I called Dani back home in Belo Horizonte, and told her everything that had happened. Since she first heard about Mariana she had longed to take her out of her living hell. Her response was simple: we had to do everything to persuade the authorities that Mariana had to be taken away from her home. If they let her go, she could come back to live with us. We'd be her new family, where she could recover from her past and begin to build for herself a better future.

Medina in the poor Jequitinhonha Valley region of Brazil, 475 miles north of Rio de Janeiro.

Matt and Dean on the margins of the BR-116 near Salgueiro, Pernambuco state.

Sisters Rebeca, 15 and Milene, 12, from the Chilli Peppers in Salgueiro.

12-year-old Poliana from Medina, Minas Gerais state.

Ballet class at the Pink House.

Rita Marques, now our Pink House coordinator in Medina.

Lívia, ten, and her best friend Tatiane, 12, from the Chillies.

Girls in our Pink House learning hairdressing in the beauty salon.

The BR-116 near Feira de Santana, Bahia state.

"Leilah" when we first met her at 1.30 a.m. on the side of the BR-116 in Governador Valadares, Minas Gerais state.

12-year-old Lilian from Medina.

Pink House girls performing a dance in Medina's town square.

A road in the Chilli Peppers, Salgueiro.

Lunch in the Pink House.

The effects of the year-long drought in the north-east Sertão region.

A road in the Primavera district of Cândido Sales, Bahia state.

Meninandança´s Pink House in Medina.

At the Pink House, dance is helping to raise the girls' self-esteem.

Mara, 16, from Serrinha, Bahia state.

Dean comforting Roxa, grieving mother of 14-year-old Natiele, in Padre Paraiso, Minas Gerais state.

Precious stones being sold by the side of the BR-116 outside Padre Paraiso.

The BR-116 cuts through the remotest and poorest parts of Brazil.

Eventually I took my mobile phone and wrote a message to supporters back in England and around the world who had been following Dean's and my journey on our Facebook page. It read:

**I am in tears as I write this. We have gone into a brothel on the BR-116 near Medina and rescued Mariana, the 15-year-old who is seven months pregnant. We had to take her home, but as she arrived at her house and she heard her mum shouting names at her she just sobbed and sobbed. This time I couldn't take it, it's just shattered me. We're going to the prosecutor tomorrow to try one more time to take her away. Please pray for the words to say. I'm never giving up on this girl.**

\*\*\*

It was 9 a.m. when Dean and I arrived at the children's council office to meet up with Rita again. We hadn't spoken of Mariana during the short walk over there. Deep inside neither of us expected that she would turn up there during the morning, as we'd agreed. But as we turned around the side of the building there she was, beaming a smile, a tatty satchel packed with her belongings. We came over and she gave us a hug.

"I got up before anyone else woke up. I arrived here at 7.30. I've been waiting here since then for it to open," she said.

She then pulled out a leather-bound Bible from her bag and handed it to Dean. "Someone gave it to me when I went to Belo Horizonte for an operation when I was eight," she explained. "I've kept it ever since. I hid it from my mum so she couldn't turn the pages into smokes. I think I knew that one day God would send someone to help me. Now I want you to have it."

Dean, already recovering from one of the most emotional nights of his life, choked back emotion again as he opened the first page, where Mariana had written a message, thanking him for coming for her.

We knew, though, that there were many more hurdles still to cross. First, there was the prosecutor, who up until now had been reluctant to use the law to remove Mariana from her family against their wishes. Even then, the town's notoriously difficult judge would have to agree to the drastic measure of passing custody to Dani and me, living hundreds of miles away in the state capital. Worst of all, there was the problem of her grandmother, who had by far the strongest grip on Mariana's life. We had seen before how one word from her grandmother was enough to instantly change Mariana's mind and scupper all our attempts to take her out of there. We knew that it would take some days to get the necessary paperwork together, and until then she would have to sleep at home – where her family would try everything, even threats and possibly violence, to hold on to her.

"My grandmother?" said Mariana when we mentioned her. "She's in hospital. She started being violently sick and ended up going to the emergency room. They interned her. My mum says she's flat on her back, being fed through tubes. She's been there since Friday."

Friday was the day Dean and I arrived in Medina. It was the first time we dared to believe that, just maybe, we would succeed in taking Mariana away.

Later that morning we met with Medina's public prosecutor, and to our surprise, her attitude to taking Mariana away from her family had also completely changed. The crucial difference, she told us, was that we had found her in a known child prostitution spot, and that neither her mother nor her grandmother had reported her missing or shown any concern for her wellbeing. Dean charming her with a signed copy of his new album didn't do much harm either. But for me to become Mariana's legal guardian, I needed to get a pile of documents together, some of which – like my police records – would probably need to come from Belo Horizonte. The thought of leaving Medina without Mariana, knowing how fragile she was and how easily she could be lost, was difficult to take.

Getting my "certificate of sanity" turned out to be the easiest part. When I turned up at the town's small hospital, a good-humoured doctor took me into her room. "Right, have you found yourself throwing stones at anyone lately?" she asked, before signing me off as mentally sound.

Back at Rita's house, I discovered I could print out my Brazilian criminal records check straight from a police website, along with credit checks and other official documents. Mariana stayed with us the whole day. Despite everything she had been through, we found her to be a sweet, quiet, and thoughtful girl who just longed for a chance to live a normal life. Now that chance had come along, she was grabbing it with both hands and wasn't going to let go.

By the end of the day we'd handed over the whole file to the public prosecutor. Now we just had to wait for the judge to look through the case and make a decision. After dropping Mariana back at her house for what, we hoped, would be her last night there, I wrote another message on our Facebook page:

**Guys, amazing things are happening! Mariana's grandmother, the one who always stopped her from leaving, was taken ill the day we arrived and is in hospital. This morning Mariana got up early and arrived at the children's council saying she wanted to change her life. And this afternoon the prosecutor agreed to hand her over to us whether her mother likes it or not! Keep praying, God is hearing!**

I hadn't expected the reaction I would get from that Facebook post. Unknown to me, the first post had been shared by supporters and seen by hundreds of people all over the world. People from America to Australia were eagerly following our fight for Mariana. In those few days the number of "fans" on our Facebook page jumped by hundreds, making us realize there were so many people who cared about what happened to these girls, who would join with us in making our dream of a new Meninadança project in Medina a reality.

Medina's judge happened to be on holiday – maybe another answer to prayer – so the case was passed on to the judge in Pedra Azul, the nearest town. It took another three days until we were finally called back to the prosecutor's office to be told that he had granted our request for custody of Mariana. Dean and I were elated, but had to spend one more night in Medina because we needed to sign the guardianship document in Pedra Azul the following morning. A letter was also delivered to Mariana's mother informing her that she would be losing her parental rights because she had "violated, in a constant way, every one of Mariana's most basic human rights" and was "no longer fit to be her mother." That afternoon she turned up at the children's council, drunk and incandescent with rage.

"No one's going to take my daughter away from me!" she spat, as Mariana sat silently next to us. "You come home with me right now. How dare you leave me. I'm going get you and break your legs, you'll see!" She stormed off and later made another scene outside the prosecutor's office.

That night we booked another room in our hotel for Mariana – there was no way we were willing to leave her at home for one more night. As we walked through the town I was nervy, keeping a constant look-out around us. Mariana's bony, trembling mother might have been a pitiful sight but I knew she was also dangerous, connected to the town's drug dealers, who often despatched bothersome people in a pool of blood. Now that we had succeeded in taking her daughter away from her – her only source of income – the place didn't feel safe any more and we were counting down the hours until we could leave.

Mariana went to bed early, leaving Dean and I sitting on a sofa in the hotel reception near her door, watching football on a flickering TV. We decided to stay there until late, keeping a look-out, just in case anyone had followed us back.

"It feels like we're guarding some priceless package, like a dignitary or something," commented Dean. "It's so opposite to the way everyone else looks at her in town... they think she's worthless."

\*\*\*

The next morning we got up early and drove straight to Pedra Azul, an hour's journey north. It took five minutes for the judge to sign the papers, handing Mariana over to me as her legal guardian. We could finally breathe a sigh of relief – we'd managed to take her away. We got straight back in the car and began the long journey back to Belo Horizonte, where

Dani was excitedly making up our spare room. Mariana sat in the back, staring quietly out of the window at the rolling hills flashing by, hardly able to believe it herself.

Remembering the one last thing there was left to do, I pulled up quickly and sent off another Facebook message:

**Dear everyone, we are now leaving Medina – with Mariana! Today the judge permanently removed her mother's parental rights. We're taking her home to rebuild her life, a long way from the BR-116. She's so happy, full of hope and with her dreams intact. She's now finally out of danger, and we're thrilled to have her as part of our family.**

And Mariana's grandmother? She was finally released from hospital and sent home a few hours after we'd left Medina. She had been bed-bound and immobilized, too weak to even speak, from the day we arrived in the town to the moment we left. Coincidence? Possibly. But if you believe that God had a plan for this precious girl's life, and that he would let nothing and nobody stand in his way, then maybe not.

## Chapter 9
# Starting Again

The view from of Sugar Loaf Mountain over the shimmering Botafogo Bay was breathtaking. I was in Rio de Janeiro, in one of the city's most exclusive *churrascaria* restaurants, overlooking one of its most famous landmarks. High up behind me, the magnificent statue of Christ stood, arms outstretched, atop a towering plug of rock. And sitting on the table next to mine was Prince Harry.

It had been a week since Dean and I had returned from Medina with Mariana, a tiring twelve-hour journey through the remote dirt tracks of the Jequitinhonha Valley back to Belo Horizonte. Both of us had needed to get back to our day jobs – Dean had a gruelling schedule of shows to get through back in Canada, and I was covering the Prince's official visit to Brazil for the British newspaper, the *Mail on Sunday*.

We had hoped to be able to travel further up the motorway during that first leg of our journey, but the unexpected turn of events in Medina had meant we'd had to change our plans. We agreed to continue the trip in three months' time, when Dean knew he could convince his record company to give him some more time off.

I'd been following Harry around all morning, just in case he did something off script which might have made the news. It was the kind of job I'd done countless times back in London, working for a celebrity-soaked tabloid that thrived off public fascination with the rich and famous, and particularly the Royals. Over the next few days, along with the British press pack that had travelled with him, we would report on Harry's every move as he ran a charity fun run, played beach volleyball on Flamengo Beach and visited a community centre in one of Rio's newly pacified *favelas*. Disappointingly for us, he behaved impeccably the whole time.

While he was inside the sprawling Alemão *favela*, I heard word that a gunfight had kicked off nearby between drug gangsters and the troops that were supposed to be in control now. I quickly wrote this up and sent it to British newspapers on the newswires. The next day it was a splash in the *Daily Star*, headlined "Harry in Gun Horror".

In terms of outward appearance, my life had returned to normal… but I knew nothing would be the same again. I was with the third in line to the throne, but all I could think about was the traumatized young girls we'd left behind along the BR-116, their horrific stories never told, their young lives so insignificant that they never made even a single column inch in any newspaper. My mind never stopped as I mulled over how to make their plight known, and how we would go about doing something to show them that they were not forgotten.

Dean too, back in Canada kicking off a college tour and playing in front of thousands of screaming fans every night, was feeling the same. The night I arrived in Rio he wrote me an email:

**Just got back to the hotel… it's 1.53 a.m.**
**It was a little crazy tonight. Three songs**
**in, a fight broke out in front of us between**
**two girls. Security finally reached them**

**and pulled them out. Country fans can be wild… and the screaming unbearable! But that's why I love 'em… they're a passionate bunch.**

**I can't help but think of Brazil tonight. Two different worlds. It's definitely an adjustment travelling between them. And hard to believe that just a week ago we were travelling with Mariana on that crazy dirt road! I look forward to carrying on up the 116. I'm beginning to miss Brazil, like it's becoming part of me.**

Back in Belo Horizonte, Mariana was with Dani, settling into her new home. Our spacious, wood-floored apartment in a leafy, middle-class neighbourhood was a world away from where she had come from, but she had adapted well, helping Dani around the house and quickly winning the affections of our two-year-old, Milo. But the loneliness and absence of love which had tragically become normal for her were also evident from day one. For the first few evenings we would suddenly realize that Mariana wasn't around, then find her fast asleep in her bed. No one in her family had ever cared enough to wish her "goodnight", so she had never learned to say it, and would just take herself off to bed without a word. It was a poignant reminder of the loveless existence she had lived until now.

Another revealing moment came after a torrential rainstorm, when Mariana suddenly said, "Oh, the smell of wet earth. Whenever I smell that it makes me want to run out and eat it."

"Eat earth?" I laughed, assuming she was joking.

"Yes… why, don't you like it?" she said.

As the conversation progressed, it became clear that Mariana and her brothers really did used to dig up dirt and swallow it, presumably to stave off their childhood hunger pangs. Tragically, she just assumed it was normal and had even learned to enjoy the taste. She was completely baffled when we tried to explain that eating earth wasn't what most people did.

The clash of two worlds was also evident when we were out and about. Medina, the motorway, and the surrounding small towns was all Mariana had ever known. She had no idea what a lift was, or an escalator, and when we passed by an airport she gasped at the size of the aeroplanes on the runway – she had assumed they were tiny, having only seen them cross the skies way above her. She had never heard of McDonald's, and wasn't at all impressed when I tried to explain how the fast-food chain sold burgers and fries – it was just like every burger bar in Medina. However, she was impressed by the 3D movie Dani took her to see at the cinema. Medina didn't even have a cinema, and she never quite believed a TV that big could exist, never mind one where the images came flying out right at you!

We knew, though, that a lifetime of abuse and exploitation, at the hands of those she loved the most, would have caused untold damage to Mariana, even if the scars were buried so deep down they weren't immediately visible. Over time we started to see just how profoundly she had been affected by the injustices that had been done to her.

While at first we were amazed at how quiet, calm, and well-behaved she was, we began to realize that it was her way of dealing with her trauma, by pushing her emotions so far down that she didn't feel them any more. Despite being seven months pregnant, she never talked about her baby, never got excited when he or she kicked or moved, and never talked to the son or daughter growing inside her, like every other mother-to-be would. There were lots of tears, though. They would well up in her eyes all the time, especially when we told her how much we thought of her, and how pleased we were to have her in our family. Even when we needed to pull her up on something, like eating her vegetables or using less make-up, tears would start streaming down her cheeks: "No one's ever cared for me enough to tell me," she'd sniff.

At the same time we were shocked to discover that Mariana believed prostitution was entirely normal for a girl her age. While she was angry at her mother for not loving her, she never considered that her mother or her grandmother had committed any great wickedness by making her sell her body on the motorway. For her, and many other girls she knew, sleeping with men for money was just a normal part of growing up, something both her mother and grandmother had done and which her unborn baby, if it were a girl, would be expected to do one day too.

At first Mariana would even refer to the men who paid for her as her "boyfriends", until we explained that having a boyfriend was something entirely different to what she had been taught. She'd also told us that the father of her baby was an ex-boyfriend. In fact, it emerged, he was a man she had met for a few hours and never saw again – just another client who had used her and probably paid for her.

We began to realize that, if we were to be successful in rescuing other girls like her, we would have to tackle an entire culture which considered the abuse and exploitation of children as an ordinary, acceptable part of life.

Slowly but surely, though, Mariana started trusting us and opening up. There were times when she would sit on our bed with Dani and talk for hours about everything that had happened to her. I could hardly bear to hear her stories, which she would tell in a matter-of-fact way, but which would tear me up inside, filling me with anger at those who had so cruelly taken advantage of her. I ended up wondering how she had ever managed to even stay alive until the day we found her.

From the age of nine or ten Mariana's family had started putting pressure on her to start "working" on the motorway. "They said they did it at my age too, so I should too," she said. "They told me that's how life was. For the first few years I refused to do it, I was too ashamed, but my mum and gran never stopped pushing me, saying they'd never forgive me if I didn't. So I did. It was a friend who was already doing it who taught me how."

It was the start of a life of unimaginable abuse. Before her age had even hit double figures she had become a commodity, an object that could be sold or swapped by those who were supposed to love and protect her. Her alcoholic grandmother, she told us, used to offer her to bar owners in exchange for shots of *cachaça* rum. And when she was eleven her mother gave her over to a gang of dealers for a night to clear the drug debts she had run up.

Despite using her as currency, Mariana's mother despised her daughter. "She was so jealous that I was prettier than her," Mariana told us. "She tried to kill me a few times. One night I woke up with my mum's hands around my neck, trying to strangle me to death."

As time went by Mariana started spending more time away from home. She would travel for miles up and down the motorway, often with other girls, including Letícia and Lilian, who Dean and I had also met in Medina. They would take lifts with truck drivers, stay for days in roadside brothels, or find "boyfriends" in nightclubs and parties, always using their bodies to get what they needed. Whenever Mariana finally arrived home she would get a severe beating from her irate mother, furious not that she had been missing for so long, but that she had come back without a single real in her pocket.

It was during one of those jaunts away from home that Mariana was found during a police raid on a brothel in a town called Cândido Sales, about fifty miles away from Medina, across the border in the state of Bahia. I was still in England when Rita called to tell me how, two weeks after Mariana had gone missing, officers had caught her and another twelve-year-old girl in bed with an old man, along with a female pimp. The news confirmed Rita's worst fears, that Mariana had fallen prey to a child prostitution ring. I didn't think we'd even see her again, never mind one day be able to talk to Mariana herself about what had happened there.

"I went there with Letícia, taking a lift in a truck," she told us. "We knew there were some big parties going on in Cândido Sales, where there'd be lots of men. Letícia knew of this old guy who would let us stay in his house for as long as we wanted, as long as one of us slept with him on the first night.

"But then on the second night he wanted to do it again, with both of us, and when we refused he threw us out onto the street. We went to a nightclub, wondering where we'd sleep that night. There was an older woman at the club who must have heard us talking about it. She came up to us and said she had a nice house where we could stay if we wanted."

But when Mariana and Letícia arrived at the house, in a poor suburb on the outskirts of the town, they found it was full of men, drinking and using drugs.

"There were other girls there too, the same age as us. The woman said we needed to sleep with some of the men. It was on the second night that the police turned up, but most of the men managed to escape out the back. We were taken to the children's councillor, who drove me back to Medina.

"When they delivered me home, my mother acted like she was so worried about me, but when they'd gone she just wanted to know where the money was. I told her there wasn't any and she went mental, kicking me and beating me with a piece of rubber."

Even more distressing memories were to come out, including that she had been abused by three of her uncles from the age of seven – in the same bedroom where the whole family slept, including her mother and grandmother. It would have been impossible for them not to have known about it, but when Mariana told her grandmother, she chastised her for making it up. Mariana also remembered how police officers who caught her and her friends would demand sexual favours in return for not arresting them, and how she had once been taken in by a family who said they wanted to help her, only to be taken on trips and abused by her new "father".

To summarize, everyone she had ever trusted had betrayed her, reinforcing the belief instilled in her since the day she was born that she was an object to be used and discarded.

Difficult though they were to hear, Mariana's stories provided a unique insight into the lives of girls living such precarious, dangerous existences in the motorway's dark underworld. More than anything we'd heard up until then, listening to her offload those unbearably painful memories helped us understand what took girls into that life, and what kept them there. At the age where most young girls are flowering into adolescence, under the watchful eye of a protective parent, these girls were just walking out of their homes into the night, ending up hundreds of miles away, inhabiting a world of rowdy roadside bars, squalid brothels, drugs, and, above all, violent, predatory men – who all saw them as prey.

It was a world which even Dean and I were wary of stepping into, and when we'd needed to do so during our trip we'd felt exposed and in danger, as if our lives could be taken away at any moment and with little consequence. Imagine, then, what it must be like for these young girls aged eleven, twelve, thirteen, who were by all accounts completely alone in the world, insignificant and entirely disposable.

The more Mariana talked, the more I saw her as one of those precious stones plucked from deep underneath the ground in Padre Paraíso. After all she had been through, she should have been buried by the darkness by now, just like Natiele and Ana Flávia and countless other young girls who had been lost forever. Instead God had seen her, dug her out, and chosen her to shine.

\* \* \*

It was a Thursday morning when the phone rang. As Dani listened to a voice on the other end, a look of alarm spread across her face. Mariana had gone off for a regular appointment with her midwife, who had checked her and discovered that she was already in labour and the baby could be born at any minute. Amazingly, Mariana hadn't felt any pain, even as she'd walked for thirty minutes up and down hills to the clinic. We grabbed Mariana's hospital bag and rushed to collect her before threading through heavy traffic towards the hospital. Only one person was allowed to be with her at the hospital, so Dani stayed and I returned home and waited anxiously for news.

Three hours passed before Dani called to say Mariana had given birth to a beautiful baby girl – by Caesarean, as the baby had been found to be in the wrong position for a normal birth. She was tiny and scrawny, weighing just five pounds and three ounces, because of her mother's lack of nutrition during the pregnancy. Worried doctors rushed her off to a specialist unit as soon as she was born. She was expected to have to stay in an incubator, but the baby girl surprised them by her strength, and she was soon released to be with her mother.

When the time came for Mariana to meet her new born daughter for the first time, Dani came over to her bedside, cradling the wide-eyed baby in her arms. To her surprise and dismay, though, Mariana looked over at the baby girl for a few seconds, then turned around and went back to sleep.

Mariana had to stay in hospital for three days before the doctors were satisfied that her baby was strong enough to be taken home. Dani too, as Mariana's legal guardian, wasn't allowed to leave her, and had to spend three nights trying to doze on hard hospital chairs. But during this time Mariana's interest in the girl she had just given birth to remained minimal, and there were few signs of the normal, natural bond between mother and baby. Tragically, and inexplicably for Dani, who couldn't help but fall in love with the tiny, fragile new born, Mariana seemed unable to show her beautiful daughter any love or affection.

Hospital workers noticed it too, and when it came to finally taking Mariana and her baby home, the social worker only agreed to sign her out on the condition that Dani and I would be legally responsible for the baby by asking the children's judge for her custody.

Back at home, Mariana changed the girl's nappies, picked her up when she cried, and put her on her breast when she was hungry, but she never said a word to her and seemed to just be going through the motions. She seemed burdened by the little human being that had suddenly come into her life. After everything that had happened to her, we could understand how her concept of motherhood might have been distorted out of all proportion.

In the end we sat down with her and asked straight out what she felt for her daughter. Tears immediately welled up in Mariana's eyes. "I don't feel anything," she sobbed. "I don't love her, I never have. I can't. I want her to be happy, to never have to suffer like I did. But I don't want to be her mother."

The tiny baby girl gazed up at her confused, disconsolate mother, her beautiful brown eyes wide open in curiosity as Mariana's tears continued to fall. Just a few days in this world, she was unaware of Mariana's heartache. The teenager in whose belly she had grown had never known the love of a mother, and couldn't muster it up herself, no matter how hard she tried. Mariana's daughter reminded her of the past she was fleeing from, of one violent, abusive encounter out of hundreds that she desperately wanted to forget.

On Monday morning, two days after leaving hospital, we arrived at Belo Horizonte's children's court to discuss becoming Mariana's baby's legal guardians, as the hospital social worker had suggested. First, a representative of the children's judge talked with us, then with Mariana alone. The idea was for us to become legally responsible for the baby while we helped Mariana care for her and learn how to love her. But as she left the room in floods of tears, being helped back to her seat by the woman who had been examining her case, we knew that something was wrong. Mariana had made it clear in her interview that she didn't want to keep her baby, and, the woman explained, the judge had a responsibility to take the child away immediately.

Dani jumped up, suddenly alarmed. "No, you can't do that! We can look after her. If Mariana doesn't want her, we'll have her…"

"I'm afraid the law doesn't allow it. There's a list of couples wanting to adopt a new born baby. The baby will go to the first on the list."

At that Dani broke down in tears, imploring the woman to let her take the baby home. Dani had been the first to hold the baby girl and had spent the most time with her, cuddling her and softly talking to her. Even as we had walked up the stairs to the judge's offices she had been the one gently cradling her, worrying if she was warm enough or hungry. And now she was being told to just leave her behind, to hand her over to a court clerk and walk away.

As she became more upset, a barrister who had been hearing the commotion came over and put her arms around Dani, explaining why letting the baby go would be best.

Mariana, too, was still crying; even though she knew she couldn't be the mother she should be, she was still devastated at the thought of having to say goodbye to the daughter she had only known for five days.

Mariana and Dani both sobbed all the way back home. As I opened the front door, Mariana ran into her bedroom and threw herself on her bed, whimpering, as I quickly dismantled the cot and took away the baby clothes, toys and other reminders that had adorned the room.

It seemed to me so unfair that a girl her age would even have to make such a huge decision. Up until now it was the sheer magnitude of child prostitution on the BR-116 that had most shocked me. But now I was seeing, in my own home, how this scandal was affecting just one single life, and it was just as big a tragedy. At least Mariana was now safe and had people who wanted to help her through it. How many other young girls were out there grappling with similar feelings, forced into the darkest of corners, completely alone and utterly unprepared to deal with them?

\*\*\*

As the weeks went by Mariana rarely spoke about her baby, unless we asked her ourselves. When we did she'd say she still thought about her, but knew she'd be better off with a loving couple who could look after her. And as time went by she became more settled, came out of herself and seemed much happier. She started school, joined the church youth group and began earning pocket money helping out in a neighbour's house. We grew very fond of her – she was sweet, kind, and thoughtful, went out of her way to please us and was a playful, caring sister to Milo. On Father's Day she surprised me with a T-shirt she had secretly saved up for and a card which read: "Matt, you're very special to me. You'll always be the dad I always wanted. Kisses, Mariana."

Meanwhile, Dean and I pressed ahead with our plans to reach out to more of Medina's young girls. Rita had been tasked with finding a house in the town which would be a reference point for the girls, where they could take part in dance and other activities and where they could find help. Over the following weeks she found a number of buildings to rent in the town, but none were quite right – some too small, others too far away from many of the girls' houses, and none with a space big enough to teach dance. We began looking for plots of land for sale in the town that might allow us to construct the building we wanted.

Back in the UK, Charlotte Piek had come on board as our UK coordinator and was doing an incredible job connecting with supporters, speaking in churches, schools, and workplaces, and getting more people on board. We'd been taken by surprise at the number of people who started getting in touch, having heard about our journey, wanting to help rescue girls trapped in child prostitution on the BR-116. Before long I was hearing of an event happening every week – a danceathon in Newcastle, a ladies' night in Leeds, a "big summer clearout" in Bangor, a curry night in Bishops Stortford, a "24-hour Stay Awake" in Mansfield, a day of dance classes in London… Some people got sponsored to walk 116 miles, lose 116 pounds or give something up for 116 hours. It was overwhelming and incredibly humbling. It felt like a real momentum was building – a movement of people from around the world. Even though this tragedy was almost too big to comprehend, maybe together we could make a real difference.

Over in Canada, Dean launched his own foundation and started to raise money, both through events organized by fans, and through the proceeds of merchandise sales at his shows.

The project preparations had to be done around my work for the British newspapers, and my life became an interesting and sometimes bizarre combination of both. We were in the middle of negotiating buying a piece of land to build on when I was sent to Lima, Peru, by the *Daily Mail*, after the nephew of the singer Phil Collins was caught with a yacht full of cocaine. I found the remote prison where he was being held, persuaded a guard to let me inside, but then was pounced on by three other guards after the nephew, who clearly didn't want to be interviewed, got a Spanish-speaking fellow prisoner to raise the alarm, shouting that I was a journalist with a hidden camera. They broke my pen in two, then marched me through dark corridors and windowless rooms – with me imagining the worst – until finally releasing me onto the street outside. I eventually arrived back at my hotel, relieved but covered in dust – just in time for a conference call with Dean to discuss the land purchase.

Another time I had to interrupt a meeting with lawyers who were helping us set up Meninadança as a Brazilian charity to do a live interview with an Irish radio station about a kitten that had got stuck inside a car engine – a story I'd sent on the newswires earlier that day.

We'd decided against buying a piece of land in Medina after finding out how expensive it would be to build a house there, so Rita had continued the search. She eventually came across a house that seemed perfect – right on the corner of her street in the centre of Medina. The building was just a block away from the town's main square, and had five large rooms, including one which was big enough to be a dance studio.

Once we'd rented the house we had another decision to make – what colour to paint the outside walls. We agreed on pink, although I didn't specify which shade of pink. A week later Rita sent through a photo of our newly painted centre – covered in the brightest, most eye-catching pink you could imagine. It stood out from all the other buildings, and puzzled residents in Medina were soon asking what on earth that garish-coloured house was going to be. I loved it – it reminded me of Meninadança's first house for the street girls in Belo Horizonte, except it was even brighter. And from then on it was known by the same name – the Pink House.

\*\*\*

Four months after our return from Medina with Mariana, Dean was on his way back to Brazil so we could continue our journey up the BR-116. With all that was happening in Medina, there was the temptation to stop there, to concentrate our efforts on that town without travelling any further. But we knew there were more centres of child prostitution to be uncovered, and we needed to keep pressing on. Thirty miles north of Medina was the border with Bahia, a state in Brazil's north-east, the poorest and least developed region in the whole of Latin America. We knew that the further north we went, the more poverty we would find, and the greater the threat to vulnerable young lives.

After I had picked Dean up from the airport in Belo Horizonte we made our way back to Medina, where we had left off our journey last time. From there, we planned to head to Cândido Sales, a small, rural town in Bahia, on the margins of the BR-116. But first we had an important engagement. Rita had organized a cocktail party for Medina's most influential people, to explain more about our plans. We knew that having their support was vital, so we had to make a good impression.

Rita had rented a local community hall for the event, and to our surprise, when we arrived the place was full. Everyone who was anyone was there – the town's businessmen, school headteachers, police chiefs, council leaders, and even the mayor and his wife, sitting at round tables as waitresses offered plates of finger food. As the clock ticked down to starting time, the room alive with excited chatter, Dean and I began to worry. It was great that so many important people had come, but what if they didn't like what they were about to hear? What if they took offence to two foreigners turning up and apparently putting their town down? Our plans could be shot down in flames before we'd even begun.

The commotion hushed to complete silence as Rita took the microphone. She, too, seemed apprehensive as she thanked people for coming and introduced Dean and me. We showed a video which portrayed images of girls on the motorway and footage of some of the activities we wanted to do in the Pink House, and a group of girls from Rita's church did a dance presentation. Then it was my turn to speak. I hadn't planned what I was going to say, but ended up telling the whole story – how we'd arrived at Rita's house, met the town's girls, discovered for ourselves the tragic reality of their lives, and how we now wanted to help. The audience listened intently, but as I scanned their faces I couldn't make out whether they liked what they were hearing or were offended by it. After half an hour I sat down again, wondering if I'd said too much.

Next I passed to Dean, translating as he introduced himself. He too explained a little of why we were there, and shared his own impressions as a foreigner arriving in a remote Brazilian town. Then he took his guitar and began to sing, and as his deep, dulcet tones wafted across the room I could see people sit up, taken by surprise at the quality of his voice. As he rose effortlessly to a high falsetto at the end of a dreamy love song, the room burst out in spontaneous applause. At the end of his set, as the audience chanted excitedly for an encore, we could see they'd had a great night out – although we knew that winning them as Dean's fans didn't necessarily mean we'd managed to win their support of our project.

After all had been said and done, Rita got up to close the meeting, once again thanking everyone for coming, and finally asking if anyone had anything they wanted to say. There was silence as she held the microphone out, beckoning for anyone to come to the front and say what they thought. Then something happened which came as a complete surprise. First, a school headteacher came forward, thanked us for wanting to help the town's poor girls, and promised to support us in any way she could – even if that meant changing the school curriculum so we could give lessons to her students ourselves. Next, the social worker from Medina's court got up, telling us how impressed she was by our plans and that she too would help in any way she could. One by one, almost every member of the audience got up, took the microphone, and praised what they had heard, ensuring us we could count on their support.

Lastly, we gasped as the mayor of Medina, a white-haired gentleman called Josélio, got up and walked slowly towards the front. Despite the reception we'd had so far, we still didn't know what the most important – and most respected – man in the room was thinking. The room fell silent as he took the microphone, tapped it twice, then began to speak.

"I want to say, thank you, thank you so much," he said. "I have been so moved by everything that's happened tonight. We all know how much the girls of our town need help. Thank you for choosing Medina. I want you to know that we will support you in any way you need."

Then, turning around to me, he said: "And to show you how much I mean it, tonight, in front of all these witnesses, I am pledging to donate… a horse."

The room once again burst into applause, and as I turned around to Rita she was clapping furiously, open mouthed in disbelief. Wondering if she'd heard the same as me, I mouthed, "A *what*?"

"A horse," she shouted over the noise. "*Senhor* Josélio is a breeder of thoroughbreds, the second-best breeder in the whole of Brazil. People come from all over Brazil to buy his horses. One is worth tens of thousands of reals."

It was the best possible outcome, albeit a most unexpected one. Not only had our plans been endorsed by everyone who mattered, but we'd also won the full backing of the mayor – and gained a horse!

As Dean and I drove north from Medina early the next morning, still buzzing about the previous night's events, we were determined not to waste any of those heartfelt pledges of support.

## Chapter 10
# How Can She Smile?

"*Senhores* Matt and Dean, thanks for your interest, but I can categorically say we've had absolutely no cases of child prostitution in our town for, oh, at least the last ten years."

The bespectacled young man gently drummed his fingertips on his desk and raised his eyebrows, signalling he had nothing more to say. We were at the offices of CREAS, a council social services department for children at risk, on a cobblestoned backstreet of Cândido Sales, in the state of Bahia. Its coordinator, a smartly dressed young man called Clayton, had met us with a warm handshake as we'd arrived, and nodded sympathetically as we talked about child prostitution along the BR-116. We'd asked him about some of the cases he'd dealt with in the town and he seemed willing to help.

Then he made a "courtesy" call to his superiors. A fan hummed back and forth, flapping the corners of files piled high, as he listened in silence, occasionally uh-huhing in agreement. As soon as he had put the phone down, his tone had changed to outright denial.

"What, no cases at all?" I asked.

"That's correct. There may have been a few before then, but in the last ten years... none."

I closed my notebook resignedly. I knew what was happening – the same as when we'd met with the president of the state assembly in Belo Horizonte. But the powers-that-be of Cândido Sales were wrong if they thought we'd just take their word for it and move on. I knew enough about the town to be sure it wasn't any different to the other places we'd visited so far. Back home, Mariana had told us how, less than a year ago, she and her friends had found themselves lured to a brothel there which specialized in underage girls. From what she'd said, its goings on seemed to be common knowledge to residents, while her stories of the pimps and brothel owners who ensnared impressionable young girls made it seem as if child prostitution was a well-organized industry.

My conversations with Mariana weren't the only time I'd heard about Cândido Sales. The town was one of the places where Letícia, from Medina, had been found during her jaunts up and down the motorway, after being stabbed with a broken bottle by an older prostitute. Tatiane, from Padre Paraíso, had also told us how she and the tragic Ana Flávia, who was only eleven at the time, had been on their way there when the truck they were travelling in collided with another, in an accident which killed the driver. Both girls had to be cut free from the smashed-up wreckage, just before the entrance to the town.

Other girls we'd spoken to during our journey had also mentioned an area on the outskirts of Cândido Sales which was notorious for child prostitution. Veredinha was a poor community sprawling along the side of the BR-116, where ramshackle bars and brothels outnumbered the houses. When I Googled the name I found a newspaper report describing how, in a recent police raid, three young girls had been found in one of the seedy establishments. In the same operation, a few miles up the road, a 51-year-old bar owner was arrested after police found five underage girls – one of which they caught red-handed with a client in one of the bedrooms.

Clayton, of course, didn't know we knew this, and continued to insist his town was child prostitution free. Realizing we were wasting our time, Dean and I politely thanked him and left. As we emerged back into the bright sunlight our hearts were heavy. This was so different to what we had encountered the previous night in Medina, where everyone, even the mayor, had put their hands up to the problem. It seemed to me that by trying to camouflage what was really going on, they were playing not politics, but a dangerous game with vulnerable lives. As we wandered through the town centre's bustling streets, we wondered if we would be able to find anyone in Cândido Sales willing to tell us the truth about child prostitution here.

We decided to drop in on the town's children's council – as an elected body and part of the judicial system, it was supposed to be independent from council politics. It didn't take long to find, in another small house, almost identical to the CREAS offices. Inside, however, there was much more flurry and commotion. An old woman with a scarf wrapped around her head sat on one of the hard plastic chairs, while two young children chased each other in circles. Councillors rushed purposefully in and out. Once again we got a warm welcome, this time from a casually dressed man with a goatee called Fábio. Dean and I sat down and I explained again why we had stopped off at the town.

Fábio leaned forward over his desk.

"The lady over there," he whispered, pointing with his eyes. "She's come to take her twelve-year-old daughter home. We picked her up in the early hours of this morning selling her body to truck drivers at Ômega – that's the big petrol station on the motorway up the hill. She's in that room at the moment being interviewed by one of our team."

I translated to Dean and he shook his head despairingly. We never thought the council's official line would have been blown apart quite so soon.

"Oh, you'd be shocked by what we have to deal with here," Fábio went on. "We see them in here every week, girls who are so messed up by life, they don't care what happens to them. It's heartbreaking…"

Suddenly the door of the interview room crashed open and the girl rushed out, tears pouring down her face. She had unkempt, dyed-blonde long hair and striking brown eyes. Sobbing, she flew out onto the street, as her flustered mother quickly gathered up the children and went after her.

Fábio told us how the twelve-year-old's house backed right onto the Ômega petrol station forecourt. "Disastrous for a pretty girl like her," he said. "Her mother lost her husband and has to go out to work, and leaves the girl at home alone. She leaves the house and wanders around the truck park. It wasn't long before she was taken advantage of."

Dean asked what would happen to her.

"I imagine she'll be back here again in the next few weeks. It's tragic, but there isn't much we can do to help her. There aren't any shelters or projects we can send her to, and here at the children's council we're at full stretch. We don't even have a car. We'll just make a report and file it to the CREAS office – they're the ones who are supposed to accompany her case."

"But… that's where we were just now, and they said child prostitution doesn't exist here," I said.

Fábio smiled. "The council prefer to sweep it under the carpet. If they admit the problem exists, they'd have to spend money trying to solve it. So… they deny it."

It was a good point, and one which was beginning to fill me with fury. This town was clearly wallowing in a mire of child prostitution, and, far from having no cases in the last ten years, it was hardly coping with the number appearing each week. That confused young girl whose face had just flashed past us was one of Clayton's "non-existent" child prostitutes, who, thanks to the council's policy of denial, was unable to get the help and support she deserved. Already feeling invisible and ignored, she was being condemned to a life of misery and exploitation that would probably end in tragedy.

Child prostitution, Fábio explained, used to be unashamedly visible in Cândido Sales. Until a decade ago, it was common to see prepubescent girls waiting by the side of the motorway, thumbing for passing trucks. Since then, things had changed, he said. Firstly, as Brazil developed, such blatant displays of child sexual exploitation were no longer tolerated, with police forces obliged to intervene. Secondly, people became better off – even in small, poverty-stricken, interior towns like this one. Where once the only people with any spare money were truckers passing through, now more and more townsfolk started finding themselves with money to spend. In particular, thanks to socialist president Lula's reforms designed to eradicate poverty, the older men in the town had begun to receive pensions and other benefits.

"Just because you don't see it doesn't mean it doesn't happen," Fábio told us. "In fact it's got worse, much worse. If you want a young girl you can find her, but you need to know where to look and who you're looking for. And these days encounters are often arranged by mobile phone or on social networking sites."

Fábio lowered his voice and edged closer to us. "And you'd be shocked to find out how many men are involved, how high up it goes. There are 'big people' mixed up in this

– businessmen, politicians, policemen. Maybe that's also why the people up there don't want you digging around too much."

What Fábio was saying was certainly alarming, but I was no longer feeling as disheartened as I had been when we'd first arrived there. He was a light in that dark place, the reason why hope was still alive. All over Brazil I have found people like him – like Rita, Sônia, Abigail – passionate, courageous individuals who were making a difference where they were. Fábio, we discovered, was a committed Christian who wanted to live the gospel of the poor, to stand up for the oppressed and vulnerable – even if that put him on a collision course with those in his town who wielded all the power and influence.

As I shared my own story with him, I mentioned the new addition to our family, Mariana, and the time when she was picked up in a brothel in Cândido Sales.

"Oh yes, I remember her," said Fábio without hesitation. "The police brought her here after the raid. I was the one who drove her back to Medina. I took her straight there and arrived at three in the morning. I was met by one of the children's councillors there – now what was her name…?"

"Rita?" I asked.

"Yes, that's her."

I told Fábio she was now helping us open our project in Medina.

"It's so good to know Mariana is OK," said Fábio. "She didn't say much on the trip back, so I silently prayed for her the whole way. She seemed like such a sweet girl. God must have kept her safe in that hellish place."

I asked what the brothel was like.

"It's empty now. Do you want to see it?"

Ten minutes later we were on the outskirts of town, driving around a grid of straight red-dirt roads lined with identical brick houses with colonial-tiled roofs, the *casas populares* provided to the poorest. The simple homes had been built on a piece of unwanted barren wasteland, too steeply inclined to be of use to anyone else, between the town's open-air rubbish dump and the BR-116 motorway below. The new district had been given an attractive name, Primavera – or "Spring" – but nevertheless this was a nightmarish, neglected place. Fábio called it "*o fim do mundo*" – "the end of the world".

In one of the first roads we drove through, at the far corner of the housing project, a number of severely handicapped children and teenagers sat in the dust, rocking or staring motionless beneath the hot sun. It was the furthest road, explained Fábio, where they'd dumped all the people with mental problems. Elsewhere, small children in soiled clothes played barefoot among piles of rubble or litter that swirled in the wind, while in some places the stench from stagnant water or rotting animal carcasses was almost unbearable.

Fábio finally told me to stop in front of No. 46 in the middle of a long, straight road at the bottom of the district. To either side, matching houses – albeit each painted a different colour – stretched as far as the eye could see. The building in front of us was light pink with green windows, its walls stained by damp and faded in the sun. Nothing whatsoever would have identified this ordinary, drab house as anything more than just another humble dwelling. I wondered how many more of these inconspicuous buildings hid other dens of iniquity where children were for sale.

"It was one of the neighbours who called the police," said Fábio. "He'd see young girls being taken in here, then watch at night as dozens of men would come and go. He said it had been going on at least a year, but when drug users and other unsavoury types started turning up, he decided to report it."

The front of the house had been boarded up, so we went around the side to the back garden. I peered in through a tiny window in the back wall. The house was small and cramped, with just three rooms, each connecting to the others. The red dirt yard, which backed onto overgrown wasteland, was strewn with beer bottles, cigarette butts, and dozens of sliced-open drinks cans, used for smoking crack.

"When we arrived here this whole place was littered with used condoms and discarded girls' underwear," remembered Fábio.

He told me how, just after midnight, police forced their way into the house. The place was full of men, who scattered in the commotion, fleeing out the back door and through the wasteland. They found three young girls, the youngest aged twelve, in one of the bedrooms. Bursting into the other, officers found Mariana and another girl in bed with an older man, along with the pimp, a woman called Regina.

I asked what happened to the pimp and the man they caught in bed. "The man spent two days in jail and then they let him go, no charges. Regina was let off too – the police said she was crazy, so they couldn't prosecute her. She left Cândido Sales the day she was released. I heard she's now living in São Paulo."

"Crazy? That's not how Mariana described her," I said. "From what she said, Regina knew exactly what she was doing, she seemed completely sane."

"Oh, I'm sure it was all an act. She knew all she needed to do was pretend to be crazy and she'd get let off. Of course, she should have been examined by a doctor, but it was convenient for the police and prosecutors – one less case to deal with.

"Matt, no one is ever brought to justice in Cândio Sales, even when the abuser is caught red-handed or confesses to the crime. They just get filed away, or ripped up – who knows?

It's so disheartening, all this injustice, sometimes it makes me think about giving up. But it's also what keeps me going, if you know what I mean."

There was that word again – injustice. Nobody was punished, neither the men who came from far and wide to abuse the girls, nor the cold, calculating woman who profited from them – then pretended she was insane. She was now in another city, almost certainly doing the same thing to other impressionable young girls.

Hundreds of men in Cândido Sales, Fábio told us, were also walking free, secure in the knowledge that their sins would never be exposed, or at least never punished. And their young victims were self-destructing, because everything they saw around them confirmed what their abusers told them – that they were nothing but worthless objects. We were about to meet one of those victims.

\*\*\*

The sight took me aback at first: a child struggling under the weight of her six-month-old baby son. Lalila was fifteen, but she looked no older than ten or eleven. She looked up at us with bleary eyes, her blonde hair matted and tangled, as her chubby infant whimpered and wriggled in her tiny arms.

It was 3 p.m. when we knocked at Lalila's front door, on a wooden shack squeezed between two crumbling brick buildings, back in the main town. It was her mother who answered, and we waited outside for ten minutes as her daughter stirred and got herself out of bed. Lalila had been asleep since arriving back home at 6 a.m. this morning, her mother told us, after escaping out of her bedroom window sometime before midnight. It was what she did every day – spend all night away from home, then spend all day in bed.

Fábio had filled us in on Lalila's story, and it was truly heartbreaking. For five years – since the age of ten – she had been used as a sexual object by the men of Cândido Sales, he'd told us. It all started after she'd been abused by her stepfather in her own home. Confused and traumatized, she'd been taken under the wing of an older girl, who had forced her to sleep with men for money.

Lalila's life quickly spiralled out of control. She would go missing for weeks at a time, allowing herself to be taken "like a leaf on the wind", said Fábio, never knowing – or caring – where she would end up. Last year she had been found in a prostitution house in Vitória da Conquista, the next big town north. She had become the top attraction, with men coming from miles around after word spread about the sweet young girl who could be theirs for 30 reals (£10).

Lalila was also among the girls who police found inside the Primavera brothel with Mariana, Fábio had told us. Every man in the town knew how to find her, and many had already abused her. In fact, she had got through so many married men that she now had to keep a low profile, because many betrayed wives wanted to kill her.

"She leaves home every night. Her mother has no control over her," Fábio had told us. "She sleeps with six to eight men a night. She's completely messed up. Sometimes she does it for an ice lolly or a can of Coke.

"These days Lalila's actually seen as 'used goods' around here. She doesn't get as much work as she used to in the town. That's why she goes to the motorway, or to other towns, where nobody knows her. But the life she's living now, travelling the trucker routes, is far more dangerous. I dread the day when we discover something terrible's happened to her."

It was after returning from one of her trips away that Lalila discovered she was pregnant. One of Fábio's colleagues accompanied her to hospital in Vitória da Conquista to be with her for the birth. But becoming a mother didn't cause Lalila to curb her perilous lifestyle. Once, after she disappeared for days, leaving her weeks-old son with her own mother, the frail woman accidentally dropped him, splitting his head open. The children's council were in the process of taking the baby away from her, Fábio had said.

Lalila, when she finally appeared, didn't seem a bit like the experienced town prostitute Fábio had described, the girl seen as "used goods", or the dangerous husband snatcher hated and feared by married women. She just seemed like a child. She fidgeted as we spoke, muddled her words awkwardly and still had an innocent vulnerability about her. Mostly shy and quiet, she looked at the floor and squeezed her fingers nervously with her other hand. It was only when we asked her what her greatest dream was that she became talkative, looked up, and smiled.

"I want to be a singer," she said. "I love singing. I used to sing in the church choir when I was younger. I think I've got a good voice. One day I want to be on stage, singing to thousands of people."

They could have been the words of any young girl anywhere in the world. But it was her smile that affected Dean the most. "How can she still smile?" he wondered out loud as we walked back into town and to our hotel for the night. "Every night a succession of men take her and kick that innocence out of her. And she wakes up the next morning and somehow still looks vulnerable, still manages to dream… still manages to smile. How can she do that?"

## Chapter 11
# Beginning and End

Our car skidded and slid over loose earth as we sped down the dirt track, kicking up clouds of thick red dust in our wake. The track had started ten miles away, as we'd turned off the BR-116 just after Cândido Sales. We were now deep in the bushlands of Bahia, surrounded by barren land, spiny thickets, and bone-dry trees which hadn't seen rain for months. We were heading for a rural community called Lagoa Grande (or Big Lake), which was part of the municipality of Cândido Sales. There used to be a big lake there, explained Fábio, but it had dried up decades ago.

The reason for our journey was an eleven-year-old girl called Sabrina who Fábio suspected was being initiated into a life of prostitution. He had received reports that her mother was hiring out her young daughter by the hour to outsiders, in particular a 45-year-old businessman from Minas Gerais state who would regularly come up to Bahia to buy horses for his farm.

"Whenever the man comes up, he makes this detour to her house," Fábio explained. "Neighbours say he puts the girl in his car and goes off, then brings her back two or three hours later. Her mother's out of work and dirt poor, and when he goes he always leaves her lots of money – hundreds of reals."

It was a typical case, Fábio explained, of a child starting out on the one-way road to prostitution, one that he knew would end on the BR-116, its dead-end bars, brothels, and gloomy truck parks – a life of untold suffering. The journey almost always begins at home, he said, when a girl is abused by someone close to her, such as her father or stepfather, uncle or cousin. Once plundered of any chance of a normal childhood, girls lose their way alarmingly quickly, and the trajectory of abuse widens to neighbours or acquaintances, who might give sweeteners to keep the girls quiet, like chocolate, toys, or money. And if a girl is unfortunate enough to have a mother like Sabrina's, who begins to see a way of making money from her daughter's suffering, then the next step – sex with strangers for money – is almost inevitable.

"I've seen it so many times before," worried Fábio. "The trigger is the abuse – it completely messes up their young minds. It's like once that has been taken away from them, then everything's gone. I'm sure, if we don't stop what's happening to Sabrina now, we'll see her in a few years' time on the motorway."

There wasn't one asphalted road in Lagoa Grande, and most of the dwellings were made of wood, set back on patches of red earth cordoned off with barbed wire. Sabrina's mother, an overweight woman wearing shiny hoop ear-rings and painted red fingernails, was sitting on her front step as we pulled up, and she snarled as soon as she spotted Fábio – who she knew was on her case – in the front seat.

Sabrina was wearing a purple party dress. She ran out, hugged us, chatted, and begged to have her photo taken with us. She was affectionate and bright-eyed, asked lots of questions and was fascinated to hear Dean speak his few words of Portuguese. The only time the smile fell from her face was when she stood next to her mother for a photo. Looking at the picture later, it was clear that this bright young girl was making a silent plea for help as she stared deep into the camera lens.

As we drove away from Lagoa Grande, Fábio told us how the man he suspected of abusing Sabrina had started bringing colleagues with him, and that he'd received information that the same pattern had begun happening with another girl, aged nine, from an equally poor family in the village. Dean, in particular, was finding all this hard to deal with – his daughter, Molly, wasn't far off these girls' ages. The thought of what was happening to little Sabrina when her mother knew she could get away with it was unbearable. He asked Fábio what was being done to stop this man from doing more damage.

"That's the problem," replied Fábio. "We're working out how to catch him, but the place is so remote, it's almost impossible. There's no police station in the town, so when he turns up unannounced they first have to call us, and then we have to mobilize the police here. It takes at least an hour for them to get there, if they're not doing something more important, and by then he's long gone.

"We even know his name and address, but because he lives in another state we can't just go there and arrest him. We'd have to make representations to the prosecution service over in Minas state, which requires a whole load of paperwork and, most importantly, evidence."

It was another example of how, despite the rhetoric, Brazil falls way short of the mark when it comes to protecting its children. There always seem to be so many obstacles to what is proudly enshrined in the country's constitution – to protect children from exploitation as an "absolute priority". In this case it was a trivial bureaucratic point which allowed a child abuser to escape justice just because he lived thirty miles away across an imaginary line.

I guessed it wasn't the only reason, because I was sure a state border wouldn't have stopped police arresting someone else for a different crime, perhaps one they had more interest in solving. Until every authority in Brazil sees children, no matter who they are, as an "absolute priority", then the protection promised to girls like Sabrina will continue to exist on paper only.

\*\*\*

Night fell suddenly, enveloping us in a blackness that our headlights barely managed to penetrate as we headed back down the narrow dirt track towards the BR-116. Eventually we emerged into the light of the motorway, joining the torrent of transport trucks bombing down a long decline in the direction of Cândido Sales. Soon after, the traffic slowed as the road curled round a steep hillside, lit up with hundreds of flickering lights. It was Veredinha, Fábio said, that poor community I'd heard about previously, mentioned so many times in the same breath as child prostitution. Sure enough, at the bottom of the hill, poorly lit, ramshackle bars spilled out onto the motorway's edge. We decided to stop and find out what we could.

We left the car further down the hill and approached on foot. For a place of such notoriety, the row of shabby bars seemed strangely deserted. Most were open but empty, their owners cutting forlorn figures as they stood at the entrances staring out. On the concrete steps outside, a few figures stood or crouched in the shadows. The air seemed heavy with apprehension.

We sat down on a rusty metal table inside one of the bars and ordered a bottle of beer and three glasses. On a picture frame behind us Jesus and Buddha floated above a dreamy pasture, while on a flickering wall-mounted TV a woman was having a slanging match with her cheating husband in the nightly *novela*. A jukebox was playing pumping *brega* music. After a few sips of beer, Fábio, who had turned his "children's councillor" T-shirt inside out, asked the bar's owner where all the girls were.

"Not so many here tonight," she mumbled, looking down as she dried glasses behind the bar. "Maybe you should come back another night."

The three of us sat alone on that table for ten minutes, not wishing to prolong our time there but knowing it would arose suspicion if we upped and left so soon. The *novela* finished, and the barmaid switched to another, where another woman was shouting at her husband. We'd just said no to a second bottle when a woman with peroxide-blonde hair hobbled in on high heels, pulled up a chair next to Dean and asked him for a gin and tonic.

Her name was Daiane, she told us. She was eighteen. She looked at least a decade older, with sallow, pockmarked skin and veins bulging out of bony, thin arms. Two of her front teeth had all but rotted away and her hands were encrusted with dirt. She knocked back her G&T in an instant and called for another. It seemed like a ritual, as if only intoxicated could she do what she believed would soon be required of her.

"You from round here?" asked Fábio.

Daiane shook her head. "Haven't seen my family since I was thirteen," she said. "That's when I ran away from home. It's been so long, I wouldn't know how to get home even if I wanted to."

"Thirteen? Didn't your family come looking for you?" I asked.

She laughed cynically. "Well, if they did they didn't look hard enough," she said, knocking back another glass and banging it down on the table.

Daiane was from a small village in the sticks near Jequié, over 100 miles away, she told us. She'd started selling her body on the motorway when she was eleven, "just to get out of the house". She didn't say any more but it was clear that, like so many of the young girls we'd met, her problems had started at home. She had been roaming the motorways ever since.

"Nope, I haven't got anyone else in this world," she said wryly. "Just the other girls, they're my family now. I don't need anyone else."

Before long two other women had come in from outside and joined us at the table. Vânia was twenty-two, and Rosana, twenty-three. Like Daiane, both looked like much older women, their stories of hardship and suffering written on their bodies, which were riddled with scars and burn marks. They also asked for shots of spirits from the bar, and as they downed more alcohol they became increasingly flirtatious, taking our hands, stroking our hair and making filthy remarks. They were particular taken with Dean, who we'd said was dumb; it wasn't the greatest cover story, but the best we had come up with in the heat of the moment to disguise the fact he was a *gringo*. And once we'd said it, he had to go along with it, even as the women teased him, ruffled his hair and pinched his cheeks.

The three women were also clearly showing signs of drug withdrawal, but they probably believed they were only one more filthy encounter from their next fix. The more we refused to readily return their advances, the more impatient they became, and the more scandalous their behaviour. It was more playful than threatening, but we eventually decided we should leave before things got out of hand, so we paid the bill and headed out towards the car. The women followed us out, shouting, screaming, and trying to tug us back as we walked away down the hill. They eventually gave up and let go, and as we drove away they waved and blew kisses before heading back to the deserted brothel bars.

Three days after we left Veredinha, Fábio called with some devastating news. Two nights later, inside that same bar, Daiane had been murdered, sprayed with bullets on the orders of a local crack dealer she owed money to. Another of the girls – Fábio didn't know which – had been shot in the stomach and leg but was going to pull through.

"That's why the place was so quiet," said Fábio. "They knew something was going to happen. The hitman could easily have come while we were there, and who knows what might have happened."

It was a tragic end to a life marked only by loneliness and pain. In reality, though, so much of poor Daiane had died a long time before she met that assassin's bullet. Her life had begun like every life, with innocence and expectation, the potential to make her mark on the world. Unfortunately for her, she'd been born into a world where being abused at home is entirely normal, and where even the justice system seems to conspire against the victims of such abuse. I imagine she was like Sabrina at her age, still trusting and ingenuous, despite already having been betrayed by those closest to her. A few years later, she was probably like Lalila, under no illusion about how cruel the world was but still capable of dreaming, and of smiling. But that was all soon pummelled out of her. By the time her life bled out of her on that bar's cold tiled floor, Daiane was long past harbouring any hope at all.

In one day Dean and I had seen the beginning and the end: a young girl unknowingly being started on the road to prostitution, and another for whom that road had come to an abrupt and terrifying end. Our hearts ached for young Sabrina, knowing the years of suffering that awaited her – and all because of some ridiculous administrative glitch. And our memories of Daiane only strengthened our determination to do something, to fan that tiny glimmer of hope that we had seen in the lives of other girls we had met, before it was snuffed out for good.

## Chapter 12
# The Cow's Head

We left Cândido Sales as dawn was breaking, knowing we had a long day's driving ahead of us as we pushed further into the state of Bahia. Even in the early morning the BR-116 roared with heavy traffic. Huge cargo trucks bore down on us from behind before screaming past inches away, making our small rental car shudder. At times we would be forced onto the hard shoulder as one truck overtook another, apparently unbothered that traffic might be travelling in the opposite direction.

The further north we drove, the hotter the sun, the sparser and drier the surroundings. The worsening poverty was evident too; wattle-and-daub cottages dotted the hillsides, while women in rag clothes trudged along the roadside, balancing bulging sacks or woven baskets on their heads. The landscape, though, was no less dramatic or beautiful; in fact it seemed to get more spectacular the further we travelled. Enormous boulders jutted out from the earth, jagged green mountains plunged into rocky ravines.

I'd never travelled along this stretch of the BR-116, but many of the names we drove past were nevertheless familiar to me, places I had read about in newspaper cuttings as I'd researched for the journey.

Vitória da Conquista, the first town we passed through, rang the most bells. Run-down motels and strip clubs lined the motorway as we entered the town, where speed bumps slowed the traffic down to a crawl. It was here, Fábio had told us, where police had found little Lalila from Cândido Sales, the top attraction in a brothel specializing in underage girls. But it wasn't the first time I'd heard of the town. I took out some of the newspaper reports I'd kept, stories that headlines would have screamed about anywhere else in the world; here, most had made no more than mere columns hidden on an inside page:

> **Police today arrested a woman accused of auctioning the virginity of a 15-year-old girl for 500 reals [£150]. The woman, a well-known pimp, recruited the girl in a rural community 30 miles outside Vitória da Conquista, and brought her to town. She was then offered in an auction to whichever of her regular clients could pay the highest price. The woman confessed to the crime, and admitted she gave just 100 reals [£30] to the adolescent, and kept the rest of the money for herself.**

> **Two men and a woman were today charged with sexual exploitation of children. Police who raided a motel beside the BR-116 caught businessman Admilson Souza, 37, with an 11-year-old girl, and truck driver Adailton Santos, 29, with a 12-year-old girl. Both men said they'd bought the girls from a local pimp called Shirlei, 28, who was**

**later located in a house with other young
girls. The woman confessed to hiring out
the children for 50 reals [£15] a time. She
would give each girl just 15 reals [£4.50].**

**A woman from Vitória da Conquista
has been arrested in Spain, accused of
international sex trafficking. Police say the
woman would recruit poor girls from rural
areas around the town, promising them
jobs as maids in Spanish families. But when
they arrived in the country they became
sex slaves. The alarm was raised after one
girl managed to escape and alerted the
authorities.**

We stopped at the children's council in Vitória da Conquista, where a councillor called Renato seemed overwhelmed by the size of the problem.

"So far this year we've received nearly a thousand separate reports of children being sexually exploited," he told us. "There are many, many pimps here who are recruiting and selling poor, underage girls. They have rich and powerful people on their books."

As we travelled further, more place names jogged my memory, like Planalto, Poções, Jequié, Milagres:

**A 23-year-old man was arrested, accused of
forcing a 14-year-old to prostitute herself
to truck drivers on the BR-116. Police in
Poções found the man with the girl on the
side of the highway after being alerted by
an anonymous caller. The teenager told**

police the man was forcing her under threat of violence to sleep with truck drivers, and he would keep all the money. The man was also found with 33 rocks of crack.

A truck driver was arrested after being caught with a 12-year-old girl in his cabin during a Federal Highway Police operation last night in the vicinity of Jequié. In the same operation, police picked up two 13-year-old girls found at two different truck parks, where they were offering themselves to drivers for the purposes of prostitution. A 30-year-old man was arrested at another truck park accused of pimping two other minors, aged 11 and 14. In the last two years federal police have picked up 229 underage girls who were being sold for sex along motorways in Bahia. Forty-nine people who were using or abusing them have been arrested.

Hundreds of young girls from the rural zones are being targeted by pimps and madams to satisfy the needs of summer tourists, an investigation has found. The girls are recruited from penniless families every summer season and taken to coastal areas where they are sold to holidaymakers, both Brazilians and foreigners, on Bahia's famous beaches.

As we drove further, we began to see signs to Feira de Santana – the second biggest city in Bahia, and another name that cropped up repeatedly. One high-profile case had shocked the town:

> **A 12-year-old schoolgirl who went missing 17 days ago has been found after escaping from her captor at a petrol station on the BR-116. The girl, called Leandra, vanished from outside her school gates, with witnesses saying they saw her go off with a woman who had been talking to her. Leandra told detectives the woman, who turned out to be a neighbour, had forced her to travel up and down the motorway, taking lifts with truckers driving along the BR-116. She said the woman told her if she didn't do what she demanded she would never see her family again.**

We were twenty miles from Feira de Santana when Dean suddenly sat up in his seat and pointed ahead of us, to a road sign which read "CABEÇA DA VACA" – or, in English, "COW'S HEAD". Sure enough, as we slowed down, dozens of brick bars lined either side of the carriageway. Sônia from Padre Paraíso had said the place, which struck fear into the hearts of girls and families there, was at some point up the highway, but we'd never expected to see the name boldly printed on a luminous government-issued road sign.

It was still light but we decided to pull over and see what we could find out. Most of the brightly coloured bars were covered in signs and paintings to lure in lonely truck drivers. One green building had a huge drawing of a naked, large-bosomed woman, next to the words, "Welcome In And Come Back Always". As we wandered past the bars, a middle-aged woman with rollers in her hair came out and called us over.

"You wanting girls?" she asked.

I was momentarily taken aback by her directness. "Er, yeah," I called back. A few people drinking on a nearby table didn't even look up.

"You're too early, love. Come back tonight, they'll all be here then."

We told her we would, got back in the car and drove on. We found a hotel for the night in Feira de Santana and, at 9 p.m., headed back to the Cow's Head. As Dean and I drove through the darkness our hearts were in our mouths. We had heard so many horror stories about this place, met families who had been destroyed by the evil that went on there, and we knew that three young sisters from Padre Paraíso, and possibly others, were probably being held captive somewhere in its maze of brothel bedrooms. And those were just the cases we'd unearthed in one small town, 400 miles from here.

As our headlights illuminated the sign ahead of us, we prepared ourselves, expecting to find it heaving with rowdy men, beer flowing, and music thumping. We decided to pretend we were road-trippers on our way to Salvador, and that Dean was a Canadian friend of mine who'd come down to spend his holidays in Brazil. We would have a drink, get talking, and discreetly make it known we were more inclined to younger girls. Maybe, just maybe, we might be introduced to those three sisters, be able to take them out of there... We took a deep breath and slowed down.

But to our surprise, the place was almost completely deserted. Most of the bars were locked shut and in darkness. There were no trucks parked up, just an old VW Beetle and a pick-up underneath a flickering street lamp. The lights were on inside just two of the bars, so we made our way over to one of them.

Inside, a man and two women sat at a table chatting, while around them two young children played, chasing each other around the room. They were the grandchildren of the bar owner, Márcia, a jolly woman who leaned on the bar, joining in the conversation. We were at first taken aback by the completely unexpected scene we found inside, but carried on with our story that we had stopped on our way to the beach in Salvador. This was clearly a brothel, but with such a family atmosphere, it was impossible to go ahead with our plan to enquire about young girls. Instead, I asked why the place was so deserted. For Dean's benefit, Márcia spoke slowly, animating her words with hand signals.

"Oh, this place used to be full every night," she said, pinching her fingers together. "These days business is really bad." She pointed her thumb down. "You know why? No more pretty girls." She cupped her hands over her chest to make imaginary breasts.

But what she was saying didn't make any sense, especially as we knew that girls were still being recruited in places like Padre Paraíso and that they were being brought here.

"Why is that?" I asked.

Márcia shrugged her shoulders. "This place used to be famous all over Brazil. Truckers would say we had the most delicious 'little chickens' on the whole motorway. Business was so good… Well, they must have gone somewhere else, I guess. These days we just get mutton dressed as lamb. Look…"

She pointed to a middle-aged woman in garish make-up sitting silently on a bar stool. Márcia looked at Dean and gave him a toothy grin.

"You want…?" she said to Dean, slapping her open hand on her clenched first – another vulgar Brazilian hand signal. "You can have her for next to nothing. I'll give you the key right now!" She chortled as she took out a bunch of keys on a rope, for the bedrooms behind the bar. Dean laughed and wagged his finger at her, another Brazilian hand signal meaning "no".

We chatted with Márcia and her family for nearly an hour in that surreal setting, a roadside brothel where children were playing, next to an old, apathetic prostitute. Dean even gave everyone a rendition of "You Are My Sunshine", which was met by claps and cheers – possibly his strangest gig ever. No other customers arrived while we were there, and when we decided it was time to leave Márcia said she'd be shutting up shop. It wasn't even 10.30 p.m. when we drove away from the Cow's Head, yet by then the whole place was deserted and in darkness. Our visit had left us with more questions than answers. Where were the girls we knew had been taken there? Why had the woman we'd spoke to earlier in the day told us the place would be full of girls? We decided to visit the nearest town, Santo Estévão, the next morning, to try to find out more.

\*\*\*

Viviane, a pleasant young children's councillor, met us with a smile and invited us into her office. She was interested to hear our information about the Cow's Head, and the woman called Gaú who had recruited unsuspecting girls in Padre Paraíso. We told her about last night's visit, and what Márcia had said about the once booming prostitution stop-off now being a virtual ghost town.

"She's right in a way. The place used to be much busier, and you'd see a lot of young girls outside the bars. But in recent years there have been more police crackdowns, so the brothel owners have made sure the underage girls aren't on show. That's why many of the truck drivers stopped stopping there.

"The place is also a major point for drugs trafficking. Sometimes, when they suspect something is up, the whole place shuts down. But that doesn't mean there isn't a problem with child prostitution there any more. It still goes on, just not underneath everyone's noses. It's all been forced underground. Maybe they got suspicious after you turned up."

Viviane took down the information about the girls from Padre Paraíso and promised to pass it on to the police. But she said her greatest concern was the hundreds of girls from her own town who were victims of abuse.

"Every week we hear of another one who has been abused at home. We don't have anywhere to take them. You're telling me of girls who might be held captive in a brothel, but we have hundreds of girls who are in just as much danger, prisoners in their own homes."

*Chapter 13*

# Enslaved

The change was sudden and dramatic. As soon as we had we left Feira de Santana's scruffy city limits, following the BR-116 northwards, the landscape turned inhospitable, barren, and lifeless, drained of all colour that wasn't a shade of reddish brown. Parched, flat scrublands, covered in low, thorny bushes, stretched out to a distant horizon on both sides. Dried-up rivers scraped across the land like scars, while entire lakes stood empty, their sun-baked mud-beds cracked into mesmerizing mosaic patterns.

We were entering the Sertão, Brazil's poorest region, and one regularly punished by drought. This year's, though, was the worst in twenty years. Even the huge cacti which towered at the sides of the road were dead and shrivelled in the sun. Most shocking, though, were the dead livestock which started appearing on the roadside – cows, horses, even goats which had died of thirst, abandoned by farmers who had run out of feed or water. On one stretch we counted eight decaying cow carcasses, almost stripped to the bone by vultures. Many poor families, too, we began hearing, were on the brink of starvation.

And yet above us foreboding black clouds hung low in the sky, seemingly threatening rain. During one stop we mentioned this to a petrol pump attendant, who sighed:

"I know, it's like God's playing a cruel joke on us. It always looks like it's going to pour down, but it never does. Sometimes it spits, but it's never enough to water the ground and make anything grow. It's been like that now for nine months."

We were heading for a place called Araçí, deep in the Sertão, where a rather mysterious contact had insisted we should visit. We were halfway there and night had already fallen by the time we passed through an urban area where the movement of traffic was slow but intense, and where rows of parked-up trucks lined the road on both sides.

We were nearly through it when Dean noticed a flash of colour darting between two transport trucks — a young girl wearing a yellow top and shorts. We turned the car round to try to find her, and saw her again, striding quickly through the narrow gap between two parked HGVs. But then she was gone, and despite our best efforts, we didn't see her again. Probably she had already climbed inside one of the countless truck cabins. She was just one of the thousands of young victims of this motorway whose voices we would never hear.

I took my phone to find out where we were. The GPS showed we were on the outskirts of Serrinha, a large town and the first in the vast Sertão. We were struck by how the town stood at the exact point where four motorways crossed: the BR-116 going north–south, and three other major highways, the BA-084, BA-409, and BA-411, going east–west. We knew that where two or more major roads converged, child prostitution tended to be a greater problem, one which could only be exacerbated by the extreme poverty. We decided to delay our trip to Araçí and stop off here.

As we took a slip road off the motorway towards the town centre to find a place to stay, we had no idea what – if anything – we would discover here. Little did we know that we had already driven past a young girl waiting alone, almost invisible, in the shadows. It would be another day before we would find her, and hear a story of abuse and exploitation more horrific than any on our whole journey so far.

\* \* \*

It was 9 a.m. and Serrinha's Municipal Market was already bustling with colours, aromas, and noisy chatter. The square around the corrugated-roofed building was packed with metal stalls that brimmed with blushing mangoes, shiny green limes and ripe tomatoes, bundles of green leaves, mini-mountains of red and green chilli peppers and curling rolls of brown tobacco. A slow-moving crowd of chatting, bartering townsfolk edged around piles of giant watermelons, *carne-de-sol* (salted beef) curing in the sun and startled, trussed-up chickens. The produce must have been brought from many miles away, certainly not from the parched, barren earth surrounding Serrinha.

Once inside the Municipal Market building, though, the atmosphere changed completely. The place was dark and dank, illuminated only by narrow shafts of sunlight which streaked through the small shuttered windows high above. No market produce was being sold here, and although the building echoed with voices and commotion, it wasn't the sound of bartering over fruit and veg, but the clinking of glasses and the banter of drinking men. There was nothing here but dozens of small bars, and even at this early hour most of their wooden stools were already occupied by men slumped over beer bottles.

The market, we'd been told, was a hotspot for prostitution in the town, where poor girls flocked like flies for the money brought in by farmers and travelling traders.

We sat down at one of the bars and ordered a beer, without any intention of actually drinking it at that time in the morning. Sure enough, as our eyes grew accustomed to the darkness, we could see female figures among the men, vivid colours among the drab greys and browns. Some were grown women, but others were clearly teenagers. One girl in a loosely-hanging orange dress rested her hand on a man's shoulder, talking nose to nose. Another, in a bright-blue top and denim shorts, strutted confidently along the damp concrete alleyways, followed by a dozen male eyes. As she passed by close to us I called her over.

Her name was Josilene, she told us. She seemed ingenuous, even though her voice and mannerisms were flirtatious, believing that we were there, like the other men, to inspect the merchandise. Her wavy, black hair was tied tightly back and she had a long scar down the left side of her face. I asked how old she was and she suddenly looked wary, then swore she was eighteen. I decided to come clean, telling her we were researching about the lives of girls like her, and could really do with her help. Her eyes lit up for a moment, perhaps at the thought that someone needed her.

"I can't right now, my friends are right over there. I'll be at home this afternoon, after the market closes. Come and see me there… I'm fifteen, by the way," she said as she skipped off, disappearing between two high piles of plastic beer cartons.

Josilene's directions served us perfectly. Her house was one of a row of red-brick shacks on a dirt track on the very edge of town, just before the BR-116 snaked off northwards into the heat-hazed distance. The busy motorway was just yards away from her front door, on the other side of a sewage-filled ditch which stank in the afternoon sun. The whole area was covered in a carpet of litter – bottles, plastic bags, tin cans, and broken glass.

Josilene at first pretended she wasn't at home, hiding behind the door as her elderly mother talked to us, before bursting out with the same youthful energy we'd seen back at the market. In a gloomy front room her younger brother played with bottle tops on the floor and an unshaven, bare-chested man, apparently drunk – her mother's new boyfriend, Josilene told us – slumped on a filthy sofa.

I asked Josilene why she'd spent the day at the market when she should have been at school, but her mother butted in before she had the chance to speak:

"Oh, there's no persuading this one, not when those so-called friends of hers come by. As soon as they appear on the street outside, she's out like a shot."

"Who are they?" I asked Josilene.

"Some older girls I know," she replied. "I know I shouldn't run away, but they tell me they won't be my friends if I don't go. I haven't got any other friends."

It wasn't just skipping school to hang out at the market, explained her mother. The girls would stop by late at night, take Josilene out of her bed, and go off to thumb for lifts on the motorway. Sometimes she would be gone for days, ending up hundreds of miles away. Josilene's "friends", it appeared, would make her pay for the journey with her own body.

"The other day I tried to stop her from going but the girls started throwing rocks at me," said her mother. "I don't know what to do. Suddenly she's gone and I don't know when I'll see her again. Then I hear she's in some dodgy place miles away, doing God-knows-what."

I asked Josilene if she liked travelling with her friends, and her face dropped.

"Oh, she loves it," her mother interrupted. "If she didn't, she wouldn't disobey me and run off with them."

"Well, it's better than staying here in this dump," answered back Josilene, clearly riled. "You never give me anything I want."

"I'll start giving to you when you stop running away."

"You won't even tell me who my dad is."

Josilene's words were completely unexpected and the room suddenly fell silent. Even her mother's half-conscious boyfriend opened his eyes to see what would happen next. Dean and I felt awkward to have been responsible for such a tender subject being brought up.

"I'll tell you when you start behaving," muttered her mother sheepishly.

Josilene hugged her legs. "I just want his name on my birth certificate," she said quietly.

"OK, then. It's José. Yes, that's right, the one from Araçí," her mother suddenly announced. Just hours after first meeting this messed-up young girl in that seedy market drinking hole, we'd found ourselves in her house at the moment when she discovered who her real father was. It was clearly something incredibly important to her, maybe the root of her problems, the reason why she allowed herself to be exploited by those false friends, because she desperately wanted to be wanted.

Josilene jumped up and ran into the back room, returning a few minutes later, her eyes swollen and red. Her mother's boyfriend had already gone back to sleep. Her mother had stayed where she was, unusually silent, her head bowed.

"When can I see him?" sniffed Josilene. Her mother shrugged her shoulders.

I turned to her. "We're going to Araçí tomorrow morning. Would you like us to take you? We'll come with you to find your father, if you want."

"Yes please, I'd like that," Josilene replied, managing a smile. Dean and I said goodbye, promising to pass by in the morning to pick up Josilene and her mother – who also wanted to come, but said she would wait nearby so she didn't have to see José. Josilene waved as we left her, looking excited that she was finally going to meet the dad who she'd yearned to know for years. Just maybe, we thought, this missing piece in her life's jigsaw might help her to find herself too, and to turn her back on the BR-116 before it was too late.

\*\*\*

If you didn't know she was there, you would never have seen her. We'd driven past her several times during our few days in Serrinha, but never noticed anything but a gloomy, locked-up car repair shop on a deserted, unlit slip road. But she was there, every night, sitting motionless on top of a low brick wall, invisible in the dark shadow cast by the building's overhang. And when we did find her, sixteen-year-old Mara's story left us utterly shattered, hardly able to take in the evil that was being inflicted upon one beautiful life.

Mara, we discovered, lived just yards away from that brick wall, with her mother and two brothers at the back of the next building along, a run-down roadside *cantina*-cum-guesthouse where local workmen or truckers would go for a cheap plate of food, or a room for the night. A steep ramp behind where Mara sat led down to a concrete car yard, her front door, and a tiny dark hovel. The cramped, windowless dwelling had been built in the under-structure of the building, in a vacant space directly below the restaurant and bedrooms.

Mara's nightmare began when she was just eleven, when her single mother would leave her alone during the day while she went out to work stitching clothes at a nearby factory. Mara would sometimes wander up to the street level, where the owner of the *cantina* – a man called Jonas – would give her food. Perhaps in Jonas' warped mind that gave him the right to abuse her, threatening to throw Mara and her family out onto the street if she told.

It wasn't long before he began selling her to men renting rooms in the guesthouse, beating her if she didn't do everything they had paid for. She was, after all, his tenant, a pretty young girl, already captive to his threats, who could be ordered upstairs at any moment. She became a virtual slave. The abuse, the threats, the beatings, and the countless violent rapes continued for years – completely unbeknown to her mother.

Then nearly two years ago, when Mara had just turned fifteen, she went missing from home. As the hours turned into days her mother became increasingly desperate and called the police, who began to search nearby buildings, including the guesthouse and its bedrooms. Hearing whimpers behind one locked door, they forced their way in and found Mara lying in a pool of her own blood.

She was pregnant with Jonas' baby. He had locked her in one of the rooms and told her he wouldn't let her out, or even give her food, until she'd aborted it. So that's what the terrified young girl did, using a coat-hanger, on the floor of that dingy, dark bedroom. The blood loss was causing Mara to lose consciousness and she was rushed to hospital. Jonas was arrested.

Mara was already deeply traumatized, after silently carrying the burden of abuse for so many years. But on that day her life completely unravelled.

Afterwards she ran away from the painful memories at home and squatted on her own in a derelict building on the other side of town. With her self-esteem at rock bottom, she started selling herself to any man for whatever he could pay. She eventually returned home, but by then she was addicted to drugs – the way she'd found to numb a lifetime's pain.

Mara, though, was more than a slave to her addiction. During the short time she was away from home she had become the property of the drug gangsters who had addicted her. That's why she sat on that dark wall every night, not on display like other girls, because she wasn't available to every passer-by. She was waiting for the next client who had already paid the gang in advance to abuse a pretty young teenager. And Mara knew, if she so much as moved from that spot without their permission, she was as good as dead.

It was a female officer from Serrinha, who didn't want to be named, who had told us about Mara's story. She had been there when they broke down that motel door, finding the frightened teenage girl half-conscious on that filthy bedroom floor.

"Everyone knows about her, that she is the property of the gang, but no one does anything about it," said the officer. "It's not that they're afraid of them, it's just because they don't want to make more work for themselves. It's pure laziness."

It was 6 p.m. when we arrived at the car repair garage, and found Mara already sitting on the wall, listening to music through earphones on her mobile phone. Dressed in a pink top and denim shorts, she wore black eyeliner and had arched, manicured eyebrows. She pulled an earphone out to hear us introduce ourselves, muttered that she wasn't in a mood to talk, and waved us down the ramp to her house, where her mother had just got home.

Her mother, it turned out, appeared to be the only one in town who didn't know how serious Mara's situation was – or at least, she had closed her eyes and ears to the truth.

"I don't know what to do, she's so disobedient," she told us. "She dropped out of school, she doesn't want to find a job. She just wants to hang out with those *malandros*. The other night two men banged on my door, demanding to know where my daughter was. They told me to tell her she had to be at the Morena Bela square at nine o'clock, or else.

"I get so worried. These people Mara's involved with, they kill without pity or mercy. I've got two sons to think about. They wouldn't think twice about killing me or them to teach her a lesson. I'm even thinking of throwing her out the house. If she wants to live dangerously, fine, but I can't put the rest of my family at risk."

At that point Mara rushed in, swept past her mother and into the next room, where she started quickly changing her clothes.

"You saying bad things about me again, mother?" she called out.

"What am I supposed to do? You don't obey me any more. All you do is shout and swear, and get up to no good with those bad types."

"Oh, mother, you don't know anything about my life."

"So are you denying you do drugs, then?"

Mara came out of the bedroom holding a tube of red lipstick. "Yeah, I admit it. I do coke and cannabis. So what?"

"I think your mother's just worried about you," I said, trying to defuse the situation. "She's afraid you might be in danger."

Mara grunted. "Well, she's right there," she said, pouting her lips as she peered into a broken mirror hung on the wall. "Most of my friends have been killed. I was there when the last one was gunned down – she died right in front of me. And yeah, next time it could be me – OK, Mother?"

Mara's mother sighed heavily and turned back to her stove, shaking her head. Mara grabbed her handbag and made for the door again. She had dolled herself up in less than five minutes. I asked where she was going, dressed up to the nines on a Friday night.

"Don't know yet," she said as she headed out into the night.

Mara's mother waited until the clomp of her daughter's high heels had faded into the distance. "It's all his fault," she whispered, pointing her finger upstairs. "Jonas ruined my daughter's life. She was a good girl, happy, without a care, before he got his grubby hands on her."

I asked what had happened to Jonas.

"Ha, nothing. That's him now, drinking with his mates. It makes me sick." As she spoke you could hear the muffled boom of men's voices on the floor above, and the clomp of footsteps on the wooden floor.

"What? He's still here? I thought he'd been arrested," I said, shocked.

"Oh yes, they arrested him, then they let him go. They said the case was with the judge, but it's been two years now, and still nothing. And there he is, carrying on with his own life like nothing happened.

"That's the worst thing. Mara has to see his face every day, listen to him shouting and drinking while she lies in her bed. No wonder she's messed up. Can you imagine what that does to her?"

As we got up to leave, I suggested to Mara's mum that her daughter was probably in much deeper trouble than she thought, that perhaps she was being taken advantage of and needed her mother's love and support more than her criticism. Tears welled up in her eyes as she nodded and told me that, deep inside, she knew it. And as Dean and I walked back up to the main road, Mara was back on the wall, waiting for the next car to pull up, and the stomach-churning order to get inside.

With her bad temper and foul language, Mara didn't act much like a victim – she'd clearly had her vulnerability beaten out of her a long time ago. But she was a victim in every sense, a slave for most of her young life, both to the men who profited from her, and now also to the unbearable memories which haunted her and crushed her spirit.

As we said goodbye and crossed the road to our car, we knew Mara would become for us a symbol of the intolerable evil on this motorway, where men choose to use their power to abuse, enslave, and exploit without mercy, while other men invested with the power to stop it choose to do absolutely nothing.

Heading back to our hotel, we had to drive back to the motorway and take a roundabout before returning along Mara's street again towards the town centre. Just before the spot where Mara was sitting there was a shaven-headed man, his bulging arms crossed, standing in the road facing us. As we drove past he deliberately caught our eye, and slowly shook his head menacingly, his eyes continuing to follow us until we could no longer see him. It was clearly a message: "Stay away, or else." It was a chilling reminder of what we were really taking on – not just the social ills and political inertia which push these young girls into prostitution, but the dangerous criminal gangs, paedophile rings, and sex traffickers who will stop at nothing to keep them there.

\*\*\*

The next morning we passed by Josilene's house as we'd promised, so we could take her to Araçí to find her long-lost father. But when her mother finally appeared she told us her daughter wasn't there. Her friends had come round late last night and convinced her to run away with them, she said. She didn't know where she'd gone or when she'd appear again.

That afternoon I got a reverse-charge call on my mobile. It was Josilene. She told me she was in Candeias, just outside Salvador, Bahia's famous capital city.

"Sorry," she said, over the noise of what sounded like a rowdy bar. "My friends wanted me to go travelling with them, so what could I do? I don't know when I'll be home. Maybe next week. Maybe I'll go and see my dad then."

## Chapter 14

# Tell the World

efore leaving Serrinha, we paid a visit to the town's children's council, where a brow-beaten young woman showed us a thick black folder – all the cases of child prostitution on the motorway they'd dealt with so far this year, she said, and they ran into the hundreds. And when we talked with her about Mara, and why those who had used and abused her over so many years were still free and unpunished, she leaned forward and lowered her voice to a whisper.

"It's nothing out of the ordinary," she said. "There was another case, of a young child who was raped. The man confessed and we passed the case to the judge, expecting him to be convicted and jailed, but months passed and nothing happened. We couldn't understand it. The man had admitted the crime, he had signed his statement of confession.

"Then one day, when the judge was giving a training day for children's councillors, one of my colleagues stood up and asked why the case was still pending and why the man was still free. The judge, who's a woman, said it was because they had lots of cases to deal with, but the councillor insisted, telling her that children should be the priority.

"You know what happened? The next day my colleague was relieved of his duties. The judge forced him out because he'd dared to stand up to her and ask why justice hadn't been done. This is the kind of thing we're dealing with here."

We did finally make it to Araçí, where we found another town gripped by an epidemic of paedophilia and prostitution. One authority in the town estimated, quite matter-of-factly, that 20 per cent of the men in the town were involved in child sexual exploitation; in a town of 60,000 people, that's around 6,000 abusers. Sixty per cent of those, he told us, were men who were retired and had found themselves with a pension to spend. It was seen as quite acceptable, he explained, for older men to pay for sex with younger girls; it was so much a part of the local culture that there was a popular *forró* song with the lyrics, "The remedy for an old horse is to eat young grass."

"Who'd want to be born a girl in a place like this?" said Dean in exasperation as we drove away from the town. "They're condemned to a life of abuse from their first breath. How many escape with their childhoods intact?"

Dean and I had already clocked up over 600 miles on this journey, yet every place we stopped at shocked us more than the last, each new story we uncovered was harder to hear than the last. And by now we had no doubt: this was no isolated case, a problem in just one town, or even something affecting a single region. It was an epidemic of child prostitution infecting every single town and village, right down to the smallest community, along this vast highway.

We also knew that what we had found so far had barely scraped the surface of the problem. For every girl like Mara there were thousands of others – enslaved, beaten, hidden away, suffering in silence. For every youngster we'd met like Josilene, running away from home to travel the dangerous trucker routes, there were countless others – traumatized, confused souls falling into the hands of paedophile gangs, traffickers, pimps, disappearing without concern or consequence. It was a scandal on a scale much greater than anything we'd ever seen or heard before, anywhere in the world.

The numbers seemed truly staggering. A recent survey by Brazil's federal highway police identified 272 "vulnerable spots" along the length of the BR-116 where underage girls were known to be sold for sex. The true numbers, they admitted, would be higher, as they only included the places indicated to them by locals, truck drivers, and others who volunteered the information. But even their most conservative estimate meant that, along the motorway's 2,819 miles, children were being bought and sold, on average, every ten miles.

Yet how many people back home had even heard of the BR-116? Even people I knew who were passionate about children's rights, who went out of their way to research and inform themselves, never included the motorway on their list of child prostitution hotspots. But just in Medina, for example, we knew there were at least 100 young girls living a nightmare of abuse and exploitation. You could multiply that number many hundreds of times along the motorway's length – a distance the equivalent of London to Tehran. We just couldn't understand how such an unprecedented tragedy had managed to stay hidden, unreported, its victims unheard and unprotected, for so long.

The last part of our journey would now have to wait until Dean was back in Brazil – he had to fly straight back to do a show in northern Canada. But in the meantime there was much to do. We decided that raising awareness of the BR-116 tragedy should be just as much a priority as working with the girls themselves. We knew the problem was too big for us to make a significant impact on our own. But if we could draw international attention to it, then that in itself could be a catalyst for change, possibly moving other organizations, churches, and charities to consider doing their own interventions; and maybe shaming the Brazilian government into doing something to tackle it.

It was with this in mind that, a month after Dean left, I embarked on a plane from Belo Horizonte to Recife, to spend a week teaching students taking a course in "Children at Risk" at the Youth With A Mission (YWAM) base there.

The group of twenty included both Brazilians and foreigners who felt called to international missions, particularly work with children. As I recounted the stories of the girls we'd met, and showed pictures and videos, many gasped in horror, while others left the room, needing to grapple on their own with what they had seen and heard. Many of the foreign YWAMers had come to Brazil knowing about the serious issues facing children, but none had ever heard about this. Even the Brazilian nationals were shocked at what was happening just half a day's journey from their front doors.

On the fourth day of teaching, Julie Gali, a Canadian who, with her husband Mati, leads YWAM's work in Recife, asked to speak to me.

"Matt, it's been so distressing to hear about what's going on on the BR-116. We all want to do something. I'd like to put a team together, see if we could start a new work in one of these towns, and try to rescue some of these poor girls you're telling us about."

I told Julie about a large town I knew about called Salgueiro, situated on the BR-116 deep inside Recife's state of Pernambuco. It was about 320 miles directly west of Recife, and Dean and I would be passing through during the last part of our journey north. We agreed to meet up there, look into the situation in the town together, and draw up a plan for a potential new YWAM outreach in the town.

I left Recife feeling a sense of optimism that, as overwhelming as this tragedy was, a movement of individuals and organizations, responding with their own actions and interventions, could bring real and lasting change.

Meanwhile, back in the UK, a growing number of people were getting on board as we sent news about our journey, and the exciting things that were beginning to happen with the Pink House in Medina. It was so encouraging to see so many people, many thousands of miles away, taking the cause to heart and doing what they could. When we organized a national awareness-raising "116 Coffee Morning" on 16 January (chosen because of the date, 1/16), over 100 people around the country organized events in their homes, churches, schools or workplaces, reaching many hundreds more. Events were even held as far afield as Switzerland, Italy, Australia, and the USA.

Other supporters took their own initiatives, putting out news on social network sites, writing articles for newspapers or webzines and even contacting churches and other groups themselves, asking if they could give a presentation. Often they were people I'd never met, who had heard about what was happening through someone else, and felt compelled to get involved.

As a journalist I was particularly keen to bring together communicators – writers, musicians, photographers, even poets and choreographers – to bring the issue to their audience in their way. One of our partnerships was with John3:30, a London-based group of artists who were making their mark among Christian youth. Moved by the stories they were hearing, they set about writing an EP of songs about child prostitution on the BR-116. The first track, written by recording artist and dance producer Van Nes, was entitled "Dear Consumer" and was meant to be a letter to the truck drivers who heartlessly abused the girls. I shivered with emotion at a song I knew would bring home the dreadful reality to thousands of new ears:

> **Sir oh Sir now hang your head,**
> **for what you've done you should be dead.**
> **You should have shown some self-control**
> **but instead you buried her soul.**
> **You say that it's her choice, her life,**
> **but you have made those desert eyes.**
> **Our God is a God of grace, yes true,**
> **but I know he's a God of justice too.**
> **These wounds they cannot be ignored;**
> **hearts of stone can be restored.**
> **Can you put your hand up and deny**
> **if there's no demand there's no supply.**
> **There is hope, there is hope left, hold on**
> **to it...**

Things were moving just as quickly in Brazil, where we were working hard to get the Pink House ready to open. We'd already chosen a board of directors and delivered the necessary documents to register the charity in Brazil. Rita, who had just qualified as a social worker, was to be in charge of the project in Medina, leading a team of people – social educators, dance teachers, and other professionals – who would work directly with the girls and their families.

I was also aware that we needed a Brazilian helping to coordinate the work on a national level, offering support to each new project as well as raising publicity and finding donors within the country. That came in the form of Warlei, a friend from Belo Horizonte who had helped begin the first Meninadança years ago when we started working with the city's street girls. Warlei was now an educationalist who helped struggling schools in Belo come up with strategies to engage their students and teachers. I was thrilled to have him back on board. In the interim he had picked up so much knowledge and experience, and he arrived bursting with enthusiasm and ideas.

The stories we had heard along the motorway had given us an insight into some of the causes behind this type of child prostitution, giving us a better understanding of how to intervene effectively. However, during one of our visits to Medina – a ten-hour overnight bus journey from Belo Horizonte – Warlei and I began to realize that just convincing the girls to change wouldn't be enough. If we wanted to make a lasting difference, we needed to come up with a way of convincing the entire town that it needed to change.

We arrived in Medina on the Day of the Evangelical, a bank holiday in the town when hundreds of members of local churches took to the street, doing noisy car processions, letting off fireworks, and holding evangelistic rallies. That night we walked down to the square, where a stage had been erected and a visiting worship band was playing in front of a huge crowd of locals. As a preacher paced up and down, shouting and waving his Bible, I looked over at the furthest end of the square, that shadowy corner where Dean and I had seen young girls waiting for clients. And there they were, in their skimpy tops and shorts, sitting on top of the low whitewashed wall – business as usual, despite the sound of praise and the shouting of hallelujahs.

"Child prostitution's just part of life here," Rita told us. "People who have grown up here don't see it like you and I do, even the Christians. Most people have stopped seeing it at all."

We decided to come up with a strategy to challenge people to rethink how they viewed child prostitution, which we called the "Changing Minds" programme. It would mean doing more than just working with the girls and their families in the Pink House. We would have to be present in every walk of life, from churches to social clubs, workplaces and schools, encouraging people to look again at their entrenched attitudes. But we knew it could be the crucial difference that might break the cycle of prostitution, saving not just one girl but generations of girls.

In preparation for the Pink House opening Rita and her team began befriending the girls they knew were immersed in a world of prostitution. One of the pillars of our work with the street girls was to become their friend first and foremost – to get down to their level, win their trust and confidence, then lift them up, and we asked the same from the team in Medina. Rita and the others did just that, taking the girls out for milkshakes, playing games, or even baking cakes with them, or just sitting with them in the square at night and chatting. Word began to get out among the girls that there was a group of people who seemed to be bothering about them, who were fun to be around, and who listened if they wanted to talk. One by one, girls started knocking on Rita's door, just to suss her out, find out if the rumours were true. Slowly, the girls began trusting her and the others in the team, opening up, sharing their hurt and fears. Seeds of hope – the possibility of a different, happier life – began to be sown in their lives.

\*\*\*

Back at home in Belo Horizonte, our "adopted daughter" Mariana was going from strength to strength. She was completely different from the closed, quiet girl who had first arrived in our house. She walked with a bounce and had a permanent smile, was always chatting and joking, and exuded a quiet confidence. But one day we received a letter from the judge in Medina requesting that we take Mariana there to see him. It was just an administrative matter, but Mariana was terrified at the thought of returning to her town.

"It's not just the bad memories," she told me. "I don't know what it might do to my head being back there. I'm scared it will mess me up again."

In fact what happened when we arrived in Medina after that long journey was incredible.

Shaking with nerves as she warily stepped off the bus, she was soon striding confidently through the streets, her head held high, as she realized that the town held no power over her, and that she would never stumble back into that life of humiliation and suffering. As she walked around some townsfolk didn't even recognize her, because she walked, talked, and looked so different to the girl they used to know. When they realized who she was people would gasp in amazement, hardly able to believe the transformation that had happened.

It did wonders for Mariana's self-esteem. But it also had a massive effect on the girls she used to hang around with, those who were still in Medina submerged in a life of prostitution and promiscuity.

One of those girls was Letícia, the thirteen-year-old whose father was desperate to stop her running away to the motorway. She had been one of Mariana's best friends and the two had travelled the motorway together. The last time Dean and I had visited Medina she had been missing, somewhere on the BR-116 on one of her perilous jaunts to roadside brothels. It was our second day in Medina when Rita called me, telling me Letícia wanted to speak to me, and was waiting for me in the town square.

When I arrived there Letícia was sitting on the wall with another girl about her age. The other girl told me her name was Sandra, and she was just fine, she didn't need anyone's help. I sat next to Letícia and asked how she was. The only other time I'd met her, in her dad's house back on our very first day in Medina, she had screwed up her face and hardly talked to us at all. This time, though, she seemed different. She told me she'd just seen Mariana, and hardly recognized her. Then she paused as a deep sadness seemed to overwhelm her.

"I want to get out of this life too," she said quietly, pulling at her hair as she looked at her feet. "Now even my dad doesn't want me in the house. I've had enough of this life. I want… help." Letícia looked as shocked as her friend standing next to her that she'd even managed to say that word.

"Letícia," I said. "The last time I spoke to your dad he told me that he doesn't even sleep when you run away from home. He said your grandmother is so sad because you're the one who helped her and kept her company. I don't think he knows what to do to get you back. But I know one thing, he really loves you."

At that tears began to fall down Letícia's cheeks. She wiped her eyes and laughed at her friend in embarrassment. But it was a breakthrough moment for this broken, messed-up young girl, the first time she had said asked someone for help, said the words out loud.

Over the coming weeks she continued to open up as our team took her under their wing, spending time getting to know her, chatting and just treating her as they would a friend, without prejudice or pretence. For a girl who had become used to either being despised and over-looked by everyone, having someone actually express an interest in her, want to know if she was OK, was a novelty in itself.

It wasn't long before Letícia's friend Sandra also knocked on Rita's door, and after her other girls who, like her, were deeply involved in prostitution. By the time the Pink House was ready to open, the team in Medina had got to know forty-eight girls, aged between eleven and sixteen, many trapped in a nightmare of abuse and exploitation. During one week they visited each of them in their homes, delivering a personalized pink invitation to be part of the Pink House, but making clear it was they who needed to take the important first step towards change – by coming themselves the following week to register. We had no idea how many, if any, of the girls would turn up. But amazingly just two days into registration week every single one of the girls we had invited had timidly knocked on the door.

Each one also got a tour of the Pink House, and the girls either became giddy with excitement or shy and embarrassed as they saw the brightly-painted walls, the multi-coloured bean bags, the personalized boxes where they could lock up their belongings, the professionally-equipped beauty salon, and the dance studio with its wall-to-wall mirror. The walls of the house were also adorned with paintings of words and phrases designed to build up the girls' self-worth. The first thing they saw as they walked in was the phrase: "You are loved. You are special. You are worthy of your dreams." Words on the wall of the dance studio read: "Don't be the girl who fell down. Be the girl who got on her feet again". And above them in a communal space upstairs between the dance studio and beauty salon were words from Jeremiah 29:11: "For I know the plans I have for you, plans to prosper you and not to harm you, plans to give you hope and a future."

A week after registration we threw a big inauguration party at a ranch outside Medina, inviting all forty-eight girls and their families. We kept the location secret, just telling the girls that a bus would be waiting for them at the Pink House at 6.30 p.m. On arriving the girls were received like VIPs, walking down a red carpet, being shown to their tables by tuxedo-ed waiters and gazing upon a mouth-watering banquet. Dean had also flown in, prior to us recommencing our journey north, and while the girls and their families tucked in he treated them to a private concert.

As we declared our first Meninadança project open, a video was played showing the photos and names of every one of the girls, along with a track which said: "Never let anyone say that you aren't loved. Even before you were born, God dreamed of you. You are beautiful, perfect in the Father's eyes". As the song played we could see the girls beginning to hope and to believe, that they were no longer alone, that there were people who wanted to help them, that they could dare to dream of a better future.

As I stood there amid the organized chaos, the pink tablecloths, lights, lanterns, and noisy chatter, I could barely contain my emotion. It had been nearly two years since Dean and I had arrived, entirely unplanned, in this small remote town, meeting Rita and hearing for the first time about how its girls were being lost like a "handful of earth falling through your fingers". It was the day we had begun to dream, of a house just for them, where they could find safety and love, where we could stop them from falling and begin to rebuild their broken lives. And here they were, those girls I'd so often wept for, gazing dreamily around at all that was happening, hardly able to believe it themselves. They included Lilian and Poliana, those cousins we'd met on the same street months ago, who had been taken off to prostitution spots on the BR-116 the next day and had seemed so far from being rescued. Fernanda, the twelve-year-old who was also at the roadside brothel when we took

Mariana away, was also there, a twinkle of expectation and hope in her eyes.

Forty-eight precious lives. When we had first come here they had been hidden away, just anonymous cases, numbers in Rita's wretched statistics. Not any more. They were all here, beaming beautiful smiles, wearing their best clothes, believing things were going to get better. We knew the real work started now, but whatever happened from this moment on we were determined to give these beautiful girls everything they longed for, and so deserved.

## Chapter 15
# Chilli Peppers

In Salgueiro, every road leads to the motorway. That's what Jordânia, a young social work student, told us as we drove through the grid of tight, dusty, cobbled streets in this large outback town in Brazil's north-eastern state of Pernambuco. She was right; numerous times over the next four days here we'd lose our way, and every time we'd just pick a road and keep driving. It was never long before the procession of back-to-back trucks roaring along the BR-116 came into view.

The other thing that happened to us repeatedly here was hearing how Salgueiro was founded. In 1835, according to the story, the three-year-old son of a Portuguese colonel went missing from their remote farm. The desperate father sent out his cowboys to search for him, promising God that if he were brought back alive, he would build a chapel in homage to his patron saint, Antônio. Two days later they found the boy, unharmed, playing underneath a willow tree – *salgueiro* in Portuguese. The colonel was so grateful, he bought the land around where his son was found and built the chapel. Slowly the town of Salgueiro began to grow up around it.

That chapel still stands, on a tidy town-centre square near a bustling open-air market. But today it is no longer the hub of life in Salgueiro. Instead, everything revolves around two interstate highways – the BR-116 and the BR-232 – which over recent decades have virtually hemmed the town in on every side. Salgueiro's strategic position had brought growth, recognition, and some wealth to the town, but, Jordânia explained, it had also made many young victims.

"Everybody here likes telling that story," said Jordânia, who had got to know many of the girls involved in prostitution in the town. "But most don't stop to consider the irony. Salgueiro was founded because a child was saved, yet today so many of our children are being lost. This time no one's sending out the cavalry to rescue them."

Dean and I had arrived in Salgueiro two days after the inauguration party in Medina, after travelling back up to the north-east region and taking up our journey from where we had last left off. Salgueiro was the next major town after Araçí, after a five-hour journey north as the BR-116 cut through the most desolate and inhospitable landscape we had encountered so far. The stretch was also the most perilous, the territory of bandits and robbers – as petrol pump attendants warned us repeatedly and with an increasing look of concern the further we went. During one ten-mile tract, either side of a narrow bridge over the São Francisco River, drivers were even advised to wait for other vehicles and travel in convoy, rather than be foolish enough to try to go it alone.

Thankfully, our only attackers were the swarms of flies and other insects that would invade our car every time we opened the door, along with the dry, suffocating heat which seemed to sap every ounce of our strength. Not one single meaningful rain shower had fallen on the north-east region of Brazil since Dean and I were last there, and the deeper we went, the fewer signs of life we found. Just in Pernambuco state over 500,000 cattle had died of thirst in the last year, pushing thousands of poor families to the brink and now making it the worst drought to have hit Brazil in the last five decades. The intense heat distorted everything, from the towering transport trucks coming over the hills towards us, to Salgueiro's townscape on a flat plain when it finally appeared on the horizon.

It was here that we had arranged to meet up with Julie and Mati, the leaders of YWAM in Recife. But almost as soon as we arrived, we got news that they and other leaders had been involved in a horrific road accident as they were travelling to a regional meeting. A car travelling at 70 mph had smashed into the back of their stationary van, sending it hurtling through the air and trapping one of them underneath while petrol poured out. Miraculously, no one was killed, but both Julie and Mati were still shaken up, and so we agreed to meet them in Salgueiro at another time.

The sun was still blazing down as we headed towards the poorest district of Salgueiro, a collection of invaded land areas called *As Pimentas* or "The Chilli Peppers", for reasons never fully explained. There were four "Chillies", Jordânia had said, each replete with social problems, broken families, addiction, and drugs-related violence. At night they turned into crime-riddled no-go areas which even the police rarely dared to enter. The uneven cobblestones which covered most of the town's streets soon gave way to red dirt tracks, lined with crumbling brick hovels or leaning wattle-and-daub shacks plastered with dried-up mud. Young children and bare-footed toddlers played amid dust, rubble, and rubbish.

"Chilli 1" was the poorest, most pitiful place Dean and I had visited so far, a living hell of squalor and brokenness baking in an insufferable heat. But after coming so far, and encountering so much tragedy along the way, we didn't think what we might find here could shock us. But we were wrong.

In the Chillies, the scourge of child prostitution seemed to have found its way into every street and, in one way or another, almost every home. In other places where we had stopped, the stories were just as heartbreaking, but never nearly as numerous. Over the next few hours we would meet over a dozen young girls, each trapped in a life of abuse and exploitation, and all within the space of less than a square mile. What was most difficult to accept, though, was their ages – the youngest was ten, and most were younger than thirteen. We would later hear from the town's children's council that there were at least 200 girls involved in prostitution in the town, and the average age was just eleven.

Some of the girls we met seemed so young Dean and I would at first wonder if we'd knocked on the wrong door. It was only after we'd made our introductions that we were sure we'd come to the right address, and with each pretty, shy girl who smiled or shook our hands our sense of horror steadily grew.

They included twelve-year-old Tatiane, who lived with her parents in a two-roomed brick house in one of the last streets in Chilli 1, just before the slum ended abruptly in a huge crocodile-filled swamp. What we'd heard was that she would spend most nights wandering the Chillies' dark dirt roads, selling her body in exchange for drugs and alcohol. The girl we met, though, was sweet and shy, dressed in her school uniform with her hair carefully tied back. She told us that her favourite thing was "drawing and colouring in".

Almost directly opposite Tatiane's house lived Lívia, a cheeky ten-year-old who arrived out of breath after leaving her friends playing football on the street outside. She was Tatiane's best friend, and was just as deeply involved in prostitution. Again, it was impossible to imagine this fresh-faced young girl flaunting herself in front of men in bars and seedy *botecos*. As

I asked her questions, she reeled with embarrassment at being put on the spot, hiding her face in her hands like my two-year-old son Milo does when he gets spoken to by someone he doesn't know.

After passing along an open sewer onto the next street, we came across eleven-year-old Natália, sitting on the steps of the bar which was also her home, and where at night she was expected to make money for her mother by sleeping with the punters. She wore an oversized T-shirt which she'd pulled down over her knees, and was drawing flowers in the dirt with her finger. "I'd really like to go back to our house in the country," she told me. "I was happier there, it was more peaceful. But my mum doesn't want to." Our conversation ended abruptly when her mother, who had been staring at us from behind a row of spirit bottles, barked for Natália to go inside.

Further down that road two sisters named Rebeca and Milene welcomed us into their home with sweet smiles. Rebeca was fifteen and Milene was twelve. They seemed like carefree, ordinary siblings as they chewed gum, balanced on one leg of their stools and drew love-hearts with a biro on each other's arms.

Again, their innocent, unfeigned appearance just didn't seem to match with the reports we'd heard about them. Rebeca was already a mother of two children, aged two and six months – both the product of cheap and degrading "programmes". Milene was already going out at night with her more experienced sister to pick up clients – "boyfriends", she called them – in the Chillies' known prostitution points. Little Milene had recently come to the attention of the town's children's council after she'd called the police on a man who had paid for sex with her but hadn't been able to penetrate, and began threatening to come back and "finish the job".

"We go out two or three times a week," said Rebecca, as if she were talking about going to the cinema or ice-cream parlour. "Most of the time we find boyfriends. But we look after ourselves, we always use condoms. Oh, apart from a couple of times," she said, looking over at her two-year-old daughter, playing in a frilly pink dress in the dirt.

"We're not prostitutes, though," she insisted. "We enjoy it, don't we, Milene?" Her younger sister just smiled shyly and kept chewing.

The sun was beginning to dip beneath the distant rocky hills as we knocked on yet another wooden door, halfway down a rutted red-dirt hill, in Chilli 2 on the opposite side of the district. Fourteen-year-old Lucinha was another of the Chilli Peppers girls who had come to the attention of the authorities, this time because of a sexually transmitted disease which was threatening the life of her eighteen-month-old daughter.

Like inside the other houses we had visited, prostitution was never mentioned explicitly during our entire conversation, just alluded to in more acceptable terms and words such as "boyfriends" and "going out". Everybody, though, including Lucinha's mother and aunty who sat in on the conversation, knew what was being spoken of. Lucinha seemed more reflective about her life than the other girls, perhaps because she had become acutely aware of its consequences. Her beautiful curly-blonde-haired girl sat on the concrete floor playing quietly with a broken plastic toy as we spoke.

I asked Lucinha how she had started "going out" at night.

"Well, we were living in a house made of mud," she started, twirling her hair with a finger. "They'd always be cutting the electricity because we couldn't afford to pay. So... my mother went to another town to try to find work, and I left home and went to live with my aunt.

"That's when I got with my first boyfriend. But some things happened which kind of messed up my head. I started drinking and smoking. I would spend days out on the streets. I got into a bit of trouble."

"How old were you?"

"Eleven. When my mother came back I came home again, but I kept spending the nights out. There wasn't enough room here, so I'd take my boyfriends back to my aunt's house."

Lucinha's mother, who up until now had been quietly listening, suddenly chimed up: "I didn't know what she was doing. She'd be gone for nights at a time. I was so worried, especially when women started saying they were going to kill her, because she was seducing their husbands."

Her aunt interrupted. "I blame the mothers," she tutted. "They never teach their daughters right from wrong. Some mothers even do these things in front of their daughters, then wonder why they're getting into trouble."

Lucinha's mother looked to the floor and didn't say a word, and it was clear there was perhaps more that *wasn't* being said in this conversation. Reading between the lines, though, her aunt appeared as guilty as her mother for pushing this bright young girl into prostitution – it was in her house where Lucinha had been initiated into prostitution and where all her "programmes" had taken place. While her mother and aunt bickered over who was to blame, the young girl whose life they had messed up was weighed down with guilt.

I asked Lucinha if she regretted getting into so much "trouble" and she nodded sadly. "I think I lost my childhood. I think I was too young to be doing those things. I got behind at school. And now I'm a mum, and I don't know if I'm really ready for that. And… well, a lot of bad things are still happening."

Dean and I stood up to leave and I thanked Lucinha and her family for welcoming us into their home. But then Lucinha jumped up on the sofa. "Wait!" she said. "There's something else I need to tell you – the most important thing."

We sat back down again and the room fell silent.

"Well," started Lucinha. "This is quite embarrassing, but... I got this other boyfriend, he was a married man, and he had this disease, and he passed it on to me. But then I ended up in the police station because of it, because of my daughter..."

"What do you mean?" I asked.

"She caught it too. It was up her bottom, and when the doctors examined her they thought she'd been abused, so they called the police."

I asked if she thought the man had abused her daughter. "Well, it appeared when she was four months old, when I was still meeting the man in my aunt's house. The doctors said there was no other way she could have caught it, but I don't believe them. I think she must have got it from me, while she was still in my tummy. I just can't bear to think..."

Lucinha said she had already had to go with her daughter to Recife, where the infant underwent an "intrusive" operation, but the disease – condyloma – had returned and spread. Another, even more serious, operation was booked for a few months' time. "They say she could die if the operation doesn't work this time," said Lucinha. "She cries in agony all the time. I feel so bad. It's all my fault."

As we walked back up the hill to our car, Dean and I were feeling overwhelmed by what we'd found in this square mile of misery. On every one of its squalid streets young girls were learning to live with a burden of hurt, trauma, and guilt that even most adults would struggle to bear. The most disturbing thing was that they *did* learn to live with it, and ended up believing prostitution was perfectly normal for any girl of ten or eleven – something they did in between doing their homework and playing with their friends in the street. Even the tiniest – like Lucinha's baby daughter – didn't escape the deep scars of that cruel adult world. The future looked desperately bleak for any girl unfortunate enough to have been born there.

*** 

Twenty-four hours after leaving the Chillies we returned there, having heard a story which confirmed our worst fears for the vulnerable young girls we'd met there.

It was Sinval, a children's councillor we'd got to know in Salgueiro, who told us about Diana, Sabrina, and Paula. The friends, aged twelve, fourteen, and sixteen, had recently left for school as normal but then vanished, triggering a desperate three-day search. In fact, the three girls had been taken from the streets of Chilli 3 and transported up the motorway, probably on the orders of a paedophile ring. And if it weren't for an astonishing chance event on their way to the state capital, Recife, they would probably have disappeared forever.

Sinval remembered: "Sabrina's mum called me and we immediately started looking for them. When I heard they'd gone off with Fátima, I feared the worst. I didn't sleep for three days and nights."

Fátima was an older prostitute, also from the Chillies, who had connections to the criminal underworld, both in Salgueiro and other towns along the motorway. And when she discovered that men planning a private orgy in a ranch twenty miles down the road were looking for three underage girls to "entertain" their guests, she knew exactly where to find them.

The girls later told Sinval how, as they were on their way to school, Fátima called Sabrina, convincing her and her two friends to bunk classes and meet her in a bar on the side of the BR-116. There, she and a transvestite prostitute plied the girls with *cachaça* rum, before telling them about a party which would be kicking off further down the motorway later that night. Before long they were facing the oncoming traffic, thumbing for a lift.

It wasn't until the girls arrived at the "party" that they discovered that they were the main attraction. But the exploitation didn't stop there. Once the party was over Fátima took the girls back to the motorway, where she began to sell them to truck drivers. For the next three days they travelled back and forth, taking dozens of vehicles, having sex with an untold number of men, with Fátima negotiating the price and pocketing the cash.

Meanwhile, Sinval and Sabrina's mother were in a frantic race against time to track them down. During the first few days, Sabrina would answer her mobile phone when her mother called, but always sounded intoxicated and almost incomprehensible. Prompted by Fátima, she would say they were in a certain bar in Salgueiro, and Sinval would immediately rush there, but find no sign of them. This happened several times until, on the third day, Sabrina's phone no longer rang at all. They later discovered why: Fátima had arranged to take the three girls all the way to Recife, 320 miles away on the coast, where she was going to sell them to a ruthless gang of people traffickers.

I'd already investigated child prostitution in Recife and found an organized criminal underworld designed to swallow up impoverished young girls without trace. One teenager I'd talked to told me how she'd been trafficked to Germany, where she was held as a sex slave, locked in a bedroom in a high-rise Stuttgart flat and forced to sleep with a constant stream of men. Others standing in the shadows at the famous Boa Viagem beachfront told how they were "owned" by gangsters who terrorized them with beatings and threats. Young Diana, Sabrina, and Paula wouldn't have stood a chance.

Sabrina's mother had no idea what was being planned for them, but she never gave up. She trawled Salgueiro's seedy bars, and eventually discovered that the girls had been heading to Cachoeirinha. She paid someone to drive her there, then heard that the girls had headed further east three days earlier. Undeterred, she carried on, but about twenty miles later traffic came to a standstill after a young man had been killed in a motorbike accident.

Sinval recalled: "She didn't know it, but a few cars behind her, Sabrina and the other girls were in the truck heading for Recife.

"A crowd had gathered around the poor soul who had died, and Sabrina got out of the truck to have a look herself. She walked straight past the car her mum was in. It was an incredible coincidence. Her mum called a policeman and they grabbed the girls, and arrested Fátima and the trucker."

What most astonished Sinval, though, was that none of the girls thought they were being taken advantage of. On the contrary, they thought their friends back home would be jealous of them for having such an exciting adventure.

He said: "When we interviewed Diana she told us those three days had been unforgettable. They actually believed that having had sex with so many strangers had given them extra street cred. That's what we're fighting against here – this warped culture where girls think that selling their bodies makes them cool, just like boys think they're cool to be selling drugs."

We met Diana, Sabrina, and Paula in Sabrina's house, up the other side of the steep hill in Chilli 3. Like the other girls we'd met here, the three friends seemed fresh-faced and carefree. They talked about which school subjects they loved or hated, laughed about a teacher who had tripped over and fallen on his face outside their classroom, and debated who was cuter – Justin Bieber or the *sertaneja* heart-throb Luan Santana.

What they didn't talk about was what they had really got up to during that three-day jaunt away from home. Sabrina insisted that none of the girls had done anything more than drink too much – possibly because her mother, sitting on the chair next to her, was frowning. She admitted they had taken "lots and lots" of lifts with truck drivers, but said none of them had wanted anything in return – a comment which even she had trouble saying convincingly, especially in front of Sinval, to whom she had previously confessed everything.

When I asked why they had run away from home, all the girls agreed: "We just wanted to see the world," they said.

Sabrina's mother put her head in her hands. "See the world?" she said despairingly. "You think the world is the side of a motorway, the inside of a truck? I was so worried! You have no idea how dangerous that motorway is. You hear of so many girls who vanish and are never seen again, or go off to the motorway and later turn up dead."

Only God knows how close these three girls came to being the next tragic item on the TV news.

\*\*\*

It was just after midday the next day when Sinval called me. "I found Fátima, the pimp who took the three girls. She's agreed to talk to you."

Half an hour later we had pulled up outside yet another of the Chillies' bars, out of which had scuttled a straw-haired woman with an aged face and scrawny, tattooed arms, stumbling on high heels in a scandalously short red dress. She jumped into the back of our car and looked around nervously, making us promise we wouldn't tell anyone in Salgueiro that she had met us – she had already received three death threats "because of these wretched girls", she said.

Bizarrely, despite being caught red-handed with the girls en route to Recife, Fátima hadn't yet been charged with any crime. The official reason was that the girls hadn't implicated her, but it was more likely the police didn't want to waste their time and effort on three wayward, unrepentant teenagers and a spent prostitute. However, knowing she was on their radar, Fátima had gone out of her way to "help" the children's council with their enquiries, acting the concerned mother figure wanting to get them back on the straight and narrow. I started by asking Fátima why she took the girls out of town.

She looked shocked. "Wait. *Take* them? I didn't take them. I was chasing after them, trying to convince them to come home."

I asked what she meant.

"I came across them in a bar here and told them, 'I'm going to call your parents and tell them you bunked off school.' But they said they were going to a party in Cachoeirinha. I was worried something would happen to them, so I went with them, to make sure they were OK – honest! That's why I was with them the whole time, trying to protect them and convince them to go home."

Clearly nothing was going to get Fátima to change her dubious cover story. I told her the girls had sworn no one ever paid them for sex, and she cackled loudly.

"And you believed them? Ha! Those girls probably can't even remember how many 'programmes' they did. Each one did it dozens of times every night. We must have taken thirty trucks during those three days.

"Then there were the bars we stopped at. Every man who saw them wanted some. The girls were so busy, they didn't even sleep. We went from Cachoeirinha to the turning to Belmonte and back again six times in one day. In one bar, three truckers paid for all three of them to do a striptease on top of a table."

Fátima's story that she was following the girls around, stopping anything bad happening to them, would have been laughable if it wasn't so serious. "And what were you doing during this time?" I asked.

"Me? I was trying to persuade them to stop and go home, but they just wouldn't listen. Sabrina even switched her mobile off so her mum couldn't bother her," she said, glancing over nervously at Sinval.

I asked Fátima how much they charged for each "programme".

"Twenty, thirty reals, sometimes less. The youngest one, Diana, lost her virginity on the first night. You know how much she sold it for? Twenty reals and a bottle of mineral water."

"How much did you make altogether?" I asked.

Fátima didn't even notice my deliberate slip. "Oh, it was a lot of money. You do the sums. If they'd have gone to Recife they would have made so much more. But… I managed to persuade them to stop and go home just in time…"

"*You* got them home?" I asked in surprise. "But I thought…"

"Oh yes, it was me who saved them. By the time Sabrina's mum found her, I'd already convinced her to go. And yet her dad still wants to kill me, saying I was going to sell her in Recife. He should be thanking me. Now everyone in the

Chillies thinks I want to snatch their daughters. You see? You try to do good, but no one appreciates it – you just get bad back. Huh!"

Rita's description of the girls being like earth falling through her fingers seemed just as apt in a place like the Chillies, where girls could be abducted, traded, and disposed of almost without anyone noticing. Sinval later told me he had no doubt that if Diana, Sabrina, and Paula had made it to Recife, their families would never have seen or heard from them again. He also told us about two other girls, aged fourteen and fifteen, who a year earlier had also left for Recife, and were both later found dead on the famous Praia de Galinhas beach.

We wondered how long it would be until little Tatiane, Lívia, and the other girls we'd met here would also fall prey to the motorway's pimps and people traffickers. Our dream was to stop the earth from falling here too. We knew we'd be back in Salgueiro one day.

## Chapter 16
# Apathy

The TV report was accompanied by dramatic music and the moustached anchor's announcement was drenched in suspense and sensationalism, but the story being told was simply heartbreaking. Police in Penaforte, a town on the BR-116 around thirty miles north of Salgueiro in the state of Ceará, had just arrested two men and two women, the reporter explained, accused of sexually exploiting a thirteen-year-old girl. Officers had swooped after receiving a tip-off that the girl was about to be sold to two men for 50 reals (£15).

The newsreel cut to footage showing two unshaven men wearing baseball caps standing with their backs to a stone-clad wall next to two women crossing their arms and pursing their lips furiously. Next, the camera showed the back of the girl, named only by her initials C.S.L.O., as the reporter, Tadeu Gomes, interviewed her. She wore a flowery single-shoulder dress and her long black hair was tied back with a butterfly clip.

The girl spoke unusually openly about her life of prostitution along the motorways of four states in Brazil's north-east. She lived a nomadic life, roaming from town to town, offering herself to truck drivers, sleeping in brothels and sex motels. She'd been in Penaforte for four days, she told the reporter, staying in the homes of two of her cousins – the women accused of pimping her. Tadeu asked how she had started out as a "programme girl".

"I started when I was ten years old. The day I came of age my mum swore at me, called me a whore and said, 'Now it's your turn.' So I started.

"My mum used to make me and my brother watch porn movies, and so I began to learn a whole load of things in life that I didn't know before. Every time she drinks she yells at us and beats us…"

The camera zoomed in on the girl biting her nails, painted a deep crimson.

"Was there any time when your mum arranged a client for you?"

"No, my clients I always found for myself."

"How much do you charge for each 'programme'?"

"Fifty reals."

"But… don't you desire to get out of this life, to leave all this?"

"Yes, I do, but I think that, you know, no one will look at me the same, people will keep reminding me of what I was, humiliating me."

The camera then switched to the four accused. The two men, who worked as odd-job men at the huge truck park in Penaforte, had been caught red-handed, arranging a threesome with the youngster for 50 reals. As the reporter interrogated them both, they said they believed the girl was over eighteen.

"But looking at her, can't you see that she's just a child?" he asked incredulously.

The two women, the girl's cousins, aged nineteen and twenty-six, had negotiated the deal and were even caught with the money the men had paid. But they too denied they had brought the girl into their home to pimp her out, claiming they were just trying to help her by giving her a place to stay. The younger woman, Rosangela, became more irate during the interview, saying: "When my husband gets out of jail – God is looking at me and knows I'm telling the truth – that girl's going to regret saying these things."

The interview with the girl continued:

"Since you started when you were ten, until today, aged thirteen, do you have an idea of how many men you've slept with?"

"I think there have been more than a hundred, including all those I didn't know – I don't even remember their faces."

A banner appeared underneath the TV screen which read: "GIRL OF 13 HAS HAD SEX WITH MORE THAN 100 MEN".

"What do you feel today?" asked the interviewer.

"Today I feel sad, because I'm something that I didn't want to be. I'm so ashamed of myself. When I walk down the street everybody looks at me, saying, 'Look, there goes the whore.' I hate it."

"And as well as doing 'programmes', do you drink, or smoke?"

"Yes, I drink and smoke, I've been doing all this since I was ten."

"You told the police that before coming here you did prostitution in Paraíba, Pernambuco..."

"Yeah, I did it there in Monteiro, then I went to Sumé, then in Sertânia. I've been to a whole load of places, doing 'programmes' at the petrol stations."

"Is your mother also a prostitute?"

"She was. I don't know if she's still doing it, because she was separated from her husband."

"How many 'programmes' do you normally do per day?"

"One day? Five. In total I make 250 reals."

"And do you regard that money as easy?"

"Yes. It's very easy for me."

"And what does that represent to you?"

"For me it doesn't represent anything, except being able to buy things for myself. And when my friends ask me, I give them the things that I've bought."

"How do you arrange the 'programmes'?"

"It's like this – the guy calls me over, asks me my name and I say, 'My name's this', and he asks, 'How much do you charge?' and I tell him, 'I charge 50,' and he says, 'Will you do it with me in the undergrowth?' and I say 'No,' so he says, 'OK, let's go to a *pousada*.' Or sometimes we go to a bar or a motel or another place. It's like that."

"You enter motels without any problem? No one asks you for your identity documents?"

"No, they don't. I go in by car, motorbike; I've even gone into a motel on foot."

"Do you know other girls the same age as you who also do 'programmes'?"

"I know lots. In Belmonte there are loads of them – Galega, Soraia, Ele, Layane, Vinha, so many."

"Don't you think it would be easier for you to study, or look for a job, rather than live this life?"

"When I get back to Belmonte that's what I'm going to do – go back to school and find work. I want to change my life, go back to how I used to be. I don't want to be this person I am today, because if I don't change, I know I won't be around for very long."

"Why?"

"Because I'm afraid that one day I'll go with a person that I don't know, he'll take me somewhere and do something bad, end up messing up my life even more. I know I can't get back everything I've already lost."

"And imagining your life from now on, what are you thinking?"

"From now on I'm going to forget this girl that I am. I'm going to go back to school, start going to church, and work for my living. I've got to do something to guarantee my future. I want to really change, put my head back in the right place."

That TV report made a big impression on me when I first watched it, nine months earlier back in Belo Horizonte. Rarely had I heard a victim of sexual exploitation on the BR-116 speak so openly and honestly about her sad existence. Facing the TV cameras, especially under the very real threats of those she had implicated, seemed like a desperate cry for help. Seeing the faces of those who had sold and bought her, and hearing their pathetic, stammering excuses, was equally disturbing.

What had happened to this messed-up young girl? Were the two men, and those foul-mouthed cousins, convicted and jailed? And was any action taken against the mother, the biggest villain of them all, who when her ten-year-old daughter most needed protecting and nurturing was handing her over to the worst types of men? Dean and I decided to find out.

Our search first took us to Penaforte, the place where the police operation had taken place. We discovered that there was a Highway Police "fiscal post" at Penaforte, where commercial drivers were obliged to stop to have their papers checked. The half-a-mile stretch of motorway was crowded with hundreds of stationary trucks, while bars and *botecos* lined the road. The place was clearly a lucrative stop for prostitutes too, judging by the number of scantily clad women we saw hobbling in between the endless rows of parked vehicles.

But if we'd entertained any illusions that the four accused might be lingering behind bars, regretting their part in the sordid affair, Edineide, a children's councillor in Penaforte, quickly ended them. They were charged and jailed, she told us, but then released on bail to await their court appearances. Very well, if the cogs of justice were still turning; the problem was, they'd ground to a complete halt. The case was close to being filed and the defendants would be acquitted.

"*Por que?*" asked Dean incredulously after I translated what Edineide had said.

"The girl, she was called Cássia, she's missing," Edineide explained. "We can't find her anywhere. I suppose she could be at any truck stop anywhere in the whole north-east. Cássia's the key witness in the case. Without her there's no point in putting any of them on trial."

It was incredibly disappointing, but tragically, not the least bit surprising. Nevertheless, Dean and I decided to keep looking for the girl, who we now knew was called Cássia. We paid a visit to the local military police barracks, and to our surprise, the police chief received us in his office, then printed off the incident report from the day, with names, addresses, and other details of everyone involved. We now had a full name for Cássia, and the names of her mother and father, and we knew they lived in São José do Belmonte, in Pernambuco.

Several hours later we were standing in front of a putrid, reeking lake in Belmonte, an isolated town at the end of a meandering long road through a sun-baked wilderness. Cássia had given her address as "Road of the Reservoir, Belmonte, Pernambuco", but we'd soon discovered that such a road didn't exist. There was a "reservoir", though – and despite the stench, the submerged chairs, floating bottles, and bags of rubbish, and the sewer pipes running into it, the stagnant lake apparently still provided water to the local community.

We began knocking on doors, asking if anyone knew Cássia, or her mother and father, but no one had heard of any of them. Maybe, Dean suggested, Cássia had made up an address to throw the authorities – and anyone else – off the scent. After almost an hour of fruitless searching, we finally admitted defeat, accepting that we wouldn't get to the bottom of this particular story.

As we drove back through Belmonte we passed the children's council building. It was Saturday, so the place was locked up, but there was a mobile number pinned to the door in case of emergencies. We decided to call to ask if Cássia had ever come to their attention. A councillor called Mislene answered, and as soon as we mentioned the girl's name she let out a knowing sigh.

"Oh yes, we know Cássia," she said. "Whenever she gets caught by the police they bring her here. But she's not from Belmonte. She has an uncle who lives here, near the reservoir, but we've also received reports that he was abusing her too. We went to his house once – it seemed more like a brothel, full of men, not the kind of environment for a young girl.

"After we saw it we never let Cássia stay there. Whenever she arrives in Belmonte we take her straight back to her mother's home."

"Where's that?" I asked.

"Conceição, in Paraíba state. She never stays there for very long, though. It's never too long before we find out she's back here again."

Not surprising, I thought, if what Cássia said about her mother was true – that she pushed her into prostitution at the age of ten by making her watch pornographic videos.

"Earlier this year Cássia was picked up by police in an old man's house here in Belmonte. There were two other girls with her, both aged eleven, and he was abusing all three. One of the eleven-year-olds later discovered she was pregnant. Again, we took Cássia back to Conceição.

"The time she was found in Penaforte was the last time I saw her. Police brought her to Belmonte because she'd told them she lived here, and we once again drove her back to Conceição. That was six months ago and I haven't heard from her since."

Later that day I called the children's councillor in Cássia's hometown of Conceição, who was also well aware of the thirteen-year-old's case.

"Everyone knows about Cássia," she said. "She's passed through the children's council more times than I can remember. Every time she gets caught somewhere she gets brought back here. It's a terrible case, isn't it? The most dysfunctional family I've ever seen."

I asked if Cássia was back at her mother's house. "I doubt it," she laughed. "That girl never stays at home for long. She hates her mother – she was the one who started her off in prostitution. The last time I heard she was back in town was a month or so ago – she's always coming or going. Once she's gone, though, nobody knows where she might be. She just gets into a truck and disappears."

I asked if Cássia's mother had been prosecuted for destroying the life of her young daughter. "It's a complicated situation," the councillor explained. "We just have Cássia's word for it, and not many judges would believe the word of a 'programme girl'. It's not as simple as you think. You need to have more evidence."

"But… she's only a 'programme girl' because of what her mother did to her. Surely…"

"Like I said, it's complicated. You have to convince a lot of people to have any chance of a conviction."

Dean and I were astonished. Less than a day after hearing

that the case against Cássia's abusers had ground to a halt because no one could find her, we had managed to discover where, at least a month ago, she had been. Her mother's home in Conceição was just sixty-five miles east of Penaforte. The fact that the children's council in Penaforte still thought she lived in Belmonte showed that no one had tried to find her so that the men who had used her, and the women who had sold her, could be tried and jailed. The biggest criminal of them all, Cássia's mother, had never been so much as questioned, let alone made to pay for what she had done to her innocent, trusting daughter. Meanwhile a messed-up thirteen-year-old girl was lost in a dangerous adult world. I remembered what Cássia had told the reporter in that TV interview – "if I don't change, I know I won't be around for very long" – and I wondered if those who had repeatedly failed to bring her justice had any idea of the consequences of their apathy and inaction.

* * *

"Police – open the door!"

Two policemen in combat gear stood either side of a metal door, backs to the wall as they took aim with their revolvers. One, a sub-machine gun slung over his back, kicked on the door with the metal toe of his boot. Behind them, four other tactical squad policemen knelt on the ground, quick-fire assault weapons at the ready.

"Open up now!" barked the officer impatiently, banging the barrel of his gun on the door. "Or we'll force our way in."

We were back in Penaforte, at the fiscal post where Cássia had been picked up with her cousins and the two men. At night the place was eerie, the huge trucks standing like menacing statues in the darkness, enveloped in a swirling mist of dust and exhaust fumes. There was also a choking stench of rotting fish – apparently a fish farm nearby had evaporated in the long drought, leaving a mountain of dead salmon and carp decomposing in the sun.

The military police chief who we had met the previous day had wanted to show us the work of his "tactical squad" in fighting child sexual exploitation in the area, so we'd arranged to meet them at 11 p.m. in the vicinity of the truck park. The policemen clearly meant business, and we were excited to be able to see the full force of the law in action – backed up with some impressive firepower – and maybe see some of the bad guys get their comeuppance.

What we had never expected, though, was what happened during the next two and a half hours.

There were signs that things weren't quite right from the very start. Dean and I had been waiting inside our car in a dark corner of the truck park, concerned not to alert anyone to a possible police action that night; we knew it could scupper the whole operation. It was 11.30 p.m. when three police 4x4s suddenly screeched into view, their bright strobe sirens flashing as they drove in convoy towards us. We transferred into one of their vehicles, and for the first ten minutes the three police cars weaved slowly through the lines of stationary trucks, illuminating the whole area and alerting everyone that the police were on patrol. Dean and I looked at each other in disbelief; if there had been anybody involved in any illegal activity, they would have been far away by now.

Along the side of the motorway, scruffy buildings lined the sides of a dark dirt track – bedrooms, one of the policemen told us, where prostitutes would take their clients. Raiding those rooms seemed like a more promising approach; they were away from the truck park and there was still a chance word of the police presence hadn't yet reached them.

But to our dismay, the soldiers parked up right at the entrance to the road, leaving their lights flashing, then started searching three men who were sitting on the street corner, doing nothing except drinking *cachaça*. It was almost as if they wanted to give anyone the opportunity to flee before they came knocking. It was another ten minutes before they moved on to the bedroom doors, banging on doors and calling on occupants to come out with their hands up.

Out of the first room came a rather sheepish truck driver, zipping up his shorts as he insisted the grisly old woman in a see-through nightie was his girlfriend, and particularly concerned whether the footage we were shooting would be shown on national TV.

After that, though, no one else opened their doors when the policemen knocked. Most of the rooms were in darkness and silent, and they simply passed them by, assuming no one was inside. Then, five doors down, a man inside shouted "What?" when they first banged on his door.

"It's the police. Open up," the soldier called back. There was no answer.

"Open the door or we'll break it down." Still the man didn't respond.

The policemen spent ten minutes trying to persuade the man to open his door, banging and shouting louder, but he had apparently decided to stay still and quiet. One of them was given a leg up so he could peer inside through the loose roof tiles, but he couldn't see anything. Another looked through the gap underneath the door, and could see the man's foot and two pairs of flip-flops lying on the concrete floor. A prostitute who was watching the drama then suggested the man had drunk too much and had fallen asleep.

"Oh, that's what it must be," said the policeman in charge. "He's probably passed out in there. Let's move on."

Dean and I were aghast. This man obviously had something to hide – why else would he have suddenly gone quiet as soon as he knew it was the police? What if he had an underage girl in there? Yet the policemen were simply taking the word of a prostitute, who could easily have been covering up for whoever was in there. If these people knew all they had to do when the "tactical squad" came knocking was to switch off their lights and say and do nothing, then these patrols weren't doing anything to combat child prostitution here. All they were doing was keeping things exactly as they were.

After knocking on a dozen other doors – all but one of which were "empty" – we got back in the police cars and did another high-visibility sweep through the truck park. Curtains twitched inside the truckers' cabins as we drove by. I asked why we weren't checking there – where most of the girls' "programmes" take place – and I was told it would cause a lot of bad feeling: most of the drivers were asleep and wouldn't appreciate being woken up so late at night.

A mile or so out of town we turned off the BR-116 into the car park of the Penaforte Motel. In Brazil motels are not places to sleep, but where couples go to have sex, and despite laws prohibiting minors, they are often places where men bring underage girls. Cássia had told the TV interviewer how most of her "programmes" were done inside motels, where owners turned a blind eye to men entering with young girls. Lights were on in the single-storey green building, which backed onto open fields. At the front a fluorescent sign flashed "Open". Like most sex motels, the entrance was a garage door which would open automatically, allowing a customer to drive straight inside and to the bedroom door, for maximum privacy.

One of the policemen knocked on the door and announced their presence, then waited for the owner to open up. The first instinct of Dean and I was to walk to the side of the building to see if we could see anyone escaping out onto the fields at the back, but the policemen just stood in front of the garage door chatting among themselves.

It was nearly ten minutes later when a man finally slid open a reception window, insisting there was no one at all in the motel bedrooms. He opened the garage door to reveal a courtyard surrounded by bedrooms, and two of the policemen started knocking on some of the doors. After the fourth door they decided to take the owner's word for it and headed back to the cars.

As we were standing there one of the policemen pointed out to me a door on the far wall of the courtyard, which opened onto the fields at the back. "You see that door, that's where the men escape when the police turn up," he said.

"Is that where they all went tonight, then?" I asked.

"Er... oh no, there was no one here tonight – didn't you hear the man tell us? It was just a quiet night – we were unlucky."

It was 2 a.m. when Dean and I left Penaforte, completely baffled by the night's bizarre turn of events. The tactical squad policemen were clearly competent and well trained, so we just couldn't understand why they would have been so lax with the job at hand – to catch those who were abusing children.

Most of the policemen, we discovered, lived in Penaforte, so maybe they just didn't want to risk putting their families in danger by upsetting those who controlled child prostitution in the town. Or maybe they, too, had been contaminated by the culture which sees young "programme girls" – whatever their age – as common prostitutes, and not worth the time and paperwork involved in picking them up.

If it was the former, we could begin to understand their unwillingness to stir things up. If it was the latter – which we rather suspected it was – then their apathy was unforgivable.

\*\*\*

The following evening we went out on another night-time patrol, this time with the children's councillors of another town on the BR-116 not far from Penaforte. This time we were confident of a better outcome. Like the police, children's councils have authority to enter bars, brothels, and other places to check if children are present; they can also demand to see IDs and make arrests. Dean and I had got to know the five members of the children's council and felt they were good, committed people who genuinely cared.

Again, we met up late at night, driving through the town's dark streets in the direction of what they told us was a notorious brothel. We parked further up the road and approached the building's flashing lights on foot, expecting to burst in and take the owner and their clientele – and any underage girls – by surprise. It wasn't long, though, before we realized that our night was going to be just as frustrating as the previous one. The councillors could have used their legal authority to walk straight in, but, just like the tactical squad the night before, they requested to speak to the brothel owner, then waited patiently on the street outside.

When the owner – a woman – finally appeared, one of the children's councillors asked to shake her hand.

"I'm so sorry to bother you," she began. "I'm here on behalf of the children's council, to congratulate you on that sign on your wall, prohibiting the entry of minors."

"Oh, thanks," said the woman. "I can assure you, I never let anyone under eighteen come into my establishment. Sometimes the young girls come and ask me to let them in, but I always refuse…"

"Well, you are doing the right thing. We need more people like you…"

Dean and I looked on in amazement. Like the military police, they were simply taking the word of the least credible of women, one who profited from prostitution and who had every interest in averting her eyes from what was really going on. As they carried on chatting, we noticed a number of girls, none of whom looked over eighteen, leaving the brothel with a crowd of others through the main door onto the street. They glanced over at the children's councillors, who were being distracted by the brothel owner's stories, and hurried away down the road into the darkness.

Our next stop was a noisy bar at the far corner of a petrol station forecourt beside the motorway. Pumping funk music filled the air, while outside inebriated men shouted and danced. Once again the councillors didn't go inside the building, which was packed with people, instead waiting outside until the owner decided to make an appearance.

"Good evening, *senhor*, we're just checking that everyone in the bar is of the legal age," said one of the councillors.

The man stood in the doorframe. "There's nobody under eighteen in here," he said abruptly.

"Right, very good. Well, thanks for your time," the councillor replied, shaking his hand and turning around back towards the car.

We were about to get back into the cars when Dean noticed a group of girls standing on the corner of a street, at the top of a steep hill directly in front of us. They seemed to be doing nothing but hanging around. From a distance, two of the girls looked very young. He pointed them out to one of the children's councillors, who glanced over and immediately dismissed his suspicions.

"No, no, I know those girls," he said. "They live there in that house. Nothing dodgy there at all."

"Wait," I said. "They do look like they're 'programme girls'. Are you sure?"

"Absolutely. I know them all – they're not prostitutes, I can assure you. Hey, do you like *forró* music? There's a live band playing on the sports field tonight – you need to see it. Come on, let's go!"

As I tried to look over in the direction of the girls, the children's councillor stood in my way, blocking my view with his head. The more he tried to avert my attention, insisting we call it a night and go to the *forró* show, the more I wanted to find out what they were really doing. I turned round and asked a man sitting on a nearby table if he knew the girls.

"Yeah, they're prostitutes," he said immediately. "They're there every night."

No longer able to ignore them, a female children's councillor walked up the hill to speak to the group of women. We watched as she introduced herself, pointing down to us as if apologetically explaining why she had had to approach them. Dean and I began to walk up the hill to meet her, but before we got there she was already on her way back down.

"Yes, they're doing prostitution, but they're all over age," she explained, waving her hands.

"But what about the two young girls?" I asked.

"Oh, it's all right, I asked about them. They said they're their daughters," she said, walking back to the car.

We didn't escape the *forró*, a type of barn dance with accordions, triangles, and men in round leather hats. As the children's councillors gleefully took to the dance floor, Dean and I tried to make sense of another perplexing night. Over the last few days we'd seen these men and women go about their work, and we knew they were genuinely interested in the welfare of girls in their town. So why would they be so reluctant to catch those who were exploiting them?

Again, could it be a fear of making enemies in their town? Or was it the result of living in a society which had become so used to child prostitution that it had lost any sense of how wrong it was? Or was it plain laziness, an willingness to make more work for themselves, especially when there was a barn dance happening at the same time?

We came to the conclusion that it was probably a combination of all these things. Child prostitution was simply part of the landscape. It took a very special person to make a stand against it, to put their reputation and career on the line to try to stop it. Thankfully, there *were* people like that in many towns and communities along the BR-116. We had met many of them, men and women who represent the hope of a different reality for generations of girls. And it would only be one more day, just up the road in the next town we visited, until we came across another.

## Chapter 17
# Untold

Jéssica woke up dazed and sore-headed, squinting in the sunlight as her blurred eyes began to focus.

The last thing she remembered was the darkness of midnight, the noises of music and chatter inside a crowded bar. Now, though, it was already day, and she could hear the drone of a diesel engine and see hills flashing past her on either side. As she came to her senses, Jéssica realized she was in the cabin of a truck which was hurtling down the motorway. As well as the truck driver, there was another sleeping girl with her, and a woman she recognized.

Jéssica didn't know it yet, but she was being trafficked, from her small town in the outback of Ceará to the state capital, Fortaleza, 315 miles away. There she would be sold to tourists on the seaside city's famous beaches. The plan was then to keep her captive, profit from her pretty innocence, then move her along the sex trafficking route – to Europe. She was only twelve.

We met Jéssica under the shade of a Jurema tree on the pavement outside her home, on one of the last streets of Brejo Santo, a small but bustling town on the edge of the BR-116. She spoke, with an innocent naivety, of her terrifying trip up the motorway to Fortaleza, a city of 2.4 million people.

Although she knew she had been taken advantage of, she clearly still didn't realize everything that had been done to her – that she had been drugged and abducted.

Jéssica admitted that, like many other local girls, she had lost her virginity at an early age, and the line between promiscuity and prostitution had quickly blurred. She and her thirteen-year-old best friend Raquel would go out at night to find "boyfriends" at nightclubs and parties, exchanging sex for rides, drinks, or sometimes money. On one particular night, the two had heard about a party in a town a few miles up the motorway, and decided to go there together.

"We were having a good time – you know, drinking, flirting, and stuff. Then a woman I knew came over – her name was Sâmia. She lived a few roads away from us and we often saw her at parties. She bought us a drink asked us if we wanted to go further up the motorway to find more parties. I can't remember what we told her, but I suppose we must have said yes, because we ended up inside a truck."

"Do you remember how you got in the truck?" I asked.

"No, but I must have been really tired because when I woke up it was already past lunchtime the next day. I never sleep so long. Raquel couldn't remember what happened either. I asked Sâmia where we were and she told us we were going to the beach."

Back home, Jéssica's mother knew that something wasn't right. While her daughter often spent nights away, she would always return home the next morning and fall into bed. When she called Jéssica's mobile, Sâmia answered. She snapped that Jéssica wasn't there and hung up. So Jéssica's mother called the police. Meanwhile, it was slowly dawning on Jéssica and Raquel that this was no innocent trip to see the famous Fortaleza sands.

"We stopped at a petrol station and I wanted to get out to use the toilet, but Sâmia and the truck driver wouldn't let me.

She said I wasn't going anywhere. I started to cry because I knew my mum would be getting worried about me, but Sâmia just told me to shut up and stay still and everything would be all right. I wasn't really frightened, because I knew Sâmia – I thought she was a nice person.

"She told us that one of us had to sleep with the truck driver, in exchange for the ride. He said he wanted the youngest, which was me. I said no way, that I didn't want to go in the first place, and that she should do it instead. Then Sâmia hit me really hard on the back and I fell on my face on the floor. So I ended up doing it. He gave Sâmia 40 reals."

It was already dark by the time they arrived in Fortaleza, Jéssica recalled. After getting down from the truck, Sâmia called the number of a man who, she told them, had a house where they would be staying, but for some reason they weren't able to go there straight away. Instead, she took the girls down to the beachfront, where, Jéssica said, there were other girls waiting in the shadows and men walking by, inspecting the merchandise.

She said: "She was threatening us the whole time, saying if we didn't do what she said we'd never see our homes and families again. She was going up to the men, telling them about us, what we'd do, and how much they'd have to pay. I went with one man and Raquel went with two.

"The other girls started making comments, saying we were taking their business. They swiped their fingers across their throats as they walked past us. I was so scared, but Sâmia told us to keep standing there. I started to cry. I thought I would never see my mum again. I didn't know what to do."

It was then that a police officer back in Brejo Santo rang Jéssica's number again. Unaware of who was calling, Sâmia answered the phone. She seemed horrified to discover the police were on her case. Finding out they were not alone also gave Jéssica and Raquel the courage to fight back, and they began to threaten to call the police themselves if she didn't take them back home. Sâmia, who was probably out of her depth, eventually gave in and found another truck to bring the girls back.

I knew something of the criminal gangs which controlled child prostitution in Fortaleza, many of which have links to international people smugglers, and I had no doubt Jéssica and Raquel had had a very narrow escape that night. Just hours after their brave fightback, the two girls would have been handed over, locked up, and started on a life of sex slavery with virtually no way out, and which could have ended anywhere in the world. During one investigation with the *Daily Mirror* I'd met Brazilian girls held as sex slaves in London, and knew that the cruelty and depravity of people traffickers knew no bounds. Jéssica and Raquel had a lucky escape – but they were the exception. Countless others wouldn't have returned to tell the tale.

I thanked Jéssica for telling me her story, suggesting it must have been painful to remember the things that had happened.

"Sort of," she said. "But that's not what hurts the most. The most difficult thing is that Sâmia wasn't even arrested. Police interviewed her after we'd got back, then let her go. She still passes me in the street as if nothing happened. She did all those bad things to me but was never punished."

Jéssica's story was so horrifying, the headlines should have been screaming about it. The fact that the woman involved was still walking free should have been a national scandal. But we were astonished to discover that this was the first time anyone had even bothered to ask Jéssica what had happened to her and her young friend during those terrifying few days just three months ago. The case hadn't even been reported by local papers in the town. And it wasn't the only appalling story of abuse and sexual exploitation we heard in Brejo Santo which had never been so much as whispered further afield.

In another recent case, a man from the town had fathered eight children – including six daughters – with his own daughter, and with the acquiescence of his wife. Only when the man began to abuse his young daughters – or granddaughters – was the case taken up by the authorities and the man jailed.

Just a few months earlier, a retired man of fifty-five was found cohabiting with two girls he called his "wives" – one was fourteen and the other twelve.

And in another case, a mother from Brejo Santo had been taking her sixteen-year-old daughter and her son's thirteen-year-old girlfriend to truck stops all over the region, where she would sell both girls for 35 reals (£10) a time. The younger girl told police she did an average of fifteen "programmes" per night, with her "mother-in-law" taking all the money. We went round to the girl's address, but her father told us she had moved away to live with relatives in another town, to try to "put the past behind her". The woman and her daughter had been arrested but had been released on bail while prosecutors decided whether to press charges. That was nine months ago.

The woman who had introduced us to Jéssica and the other cases, children's councillor Ocilene, seemed overwhelmed by the size of the problem in her town. "We've lost control," she said. "We try to do something, but it's like trying to hold back the tide. I'm so ashamed to admit it, but we no longer have control over child prostitution here.

"Most girls here think they must have an active sexual life by the time they're twelve. They think they're not normal if they're not having sex for money after they've reached puberty.

It sounds crazy, but prostitution has become fashionable among teenage girls here.

"A lot of the girls go to the fiscal post at Penaforte to sell their bodies to the truck drivers. It has got so bad, I'm preparing to make a formal petition asking for more policing at the fiscal post. The police tell us they are making regular patrols there, but it doesn't seem to make any difference.

"Sometimes I wonder where it's all going to end. We pass so many cases on to the authorities, then never hear any more about them. No one's ever punished. They just get filed away, forgotten, and everything carries on as normal. And the worst thing is, nobody ever finds out, because we're just a small, remote town which no one ever hears about. If only there were a way to tell the world what's really happening here."

Ocilene's words echoed through our minds as we drove away from Brejo Santo. We were certain that, just a few dozen miles further north, we would find more appalling cases of exploitation – untold, unpunished, deliberately forgotten. I sincerely hoped that, through the pages of this book, the voices of the girls we had met so far *would* be heard. But Ocilene was right. What about the next young girl, those childhoods that undoubtedly will be stolen tomorrow, or next week – how will anyone get to hear about them? And if no one hears, how will those girls have any hope of getting the help and the justice they deserve?

I started to think of our growing army of supporters coming together in the UK and around the world, people who *did* care what happened to these forgotten girls, who agonized over their stories and often pleaded with me to tell them what they could do to make a difference. Over the next few minutes dozens of images flashed through my mind – of stories being shared around the world, of people getting together to write letters, of thousands of postcards dropping through the letterboxes of police chiefs, prosecutors, and judges. Eventually I turned to Dean.

"Can you imagine if the judge who decided to file away Jéssica's case discovered that people all around the world knew about it? If he suddenly received thousands of letters asking what was happening with the case? Don't you think he would quickly do something about it?

"And what if we had a way of collecting the stories like Jéssica's from towns along the length of the BR-116, and got as many people as possible to hear about them? And when a judge tries to make a case disappear, what if we could deluge him with correspondence from around the world, demanding that justice be done? Surely that could make the crucial difference?"

It was the beginning of what would become an important branch of our work – Project 116 – a movement to tell the untold stories, create a tidal wave of knowledge, unite thousands in a deafening clamour for justice. It is a way for anyone, wherever they live around the world, to speak up for one individual girl, and show her and everyone else that she is not alone or forgotten, that there are people who will not let her suffering go unnoticed.

# The End – and Beginning – of the Road

We didn't even notice when the BR-116 finally came to an end. The motorway rose over a sea of terracotta roofs, swept past a shiny new airport, then split up and merged with a tangle of other roads in the centre of Fortaleza. We were soon lost in a sprawl of spiralling fly-overs, bottle-necked carriageways, and chaotic one-way streets. The motorway we'd spent a year travelling was now no more than a mention on green traffic signs.

Half a mile later we arrived at the end of Brazil itself, where a silky blue ocean lapped softly against a long crescent of golden sand, framed by skyscrapers glistening in a cloudless sky. A refreshing warm breeze ruffled the palm trees as we stood there, watching the waves gently drumming the shore, breaking and spreading and forming again. Fortaleza is the closest point in Brazil to Europe and North America – both are about 4,000 miles away, directly across the Atlantic Ocean that now lay in front of us. With the city's fast-food restaurants, shopping malls, and long promenade, we certainly felt closer to home here than we had this time yesterday, in the dust, dirt, and stifling heat of yet another poor outback town.

Later that evening Dean and I strolled to the end of a long pier which jutted out into the sea, and looked back at the brightly lit cityscape shimmering its reflection upon the gently rolling waters. This was picture-postcard Brazil, the Brazil that takes your breath away, the feel-good Brazil of sun, sea, and samba, of spontaneity, optimism, life, and colour. It is the Brazil most foreigners only ever see, and the only one that Brazil wants them to see.

But we now knew there was so much more beyond that sparkling horseshoe of hotels and high-rises – a very different Brazil, a world of pain and turmoil for thousands of innocent young girls. Few tourists lazing on Fortaleza's world-famous beaches would have any idea that, just a few city blocks behind them, is a road that for countless children has become a "highway to hell" which leads to a Brazil of darkness and despair, where childhoods are stolen and young lives are so easily shattered – with no one to pick up the pieces.

While dynamic, booming Brazil – the one we could see from that pier – concerns itself with its image and standing in the world, spending billions on car parks, hotels, and stadiums to host the World Cup and the Olympics, its vulnerable young daughters in the "other" Brazil are left abandoned and utterly unprotected. Making them an issue, of course, would reflect badly on the country just as its star is beginning to rise. It is much easier not to mention them. Some politicians even pretend they don't exist.

So the girls end up becoming victims many times over, first by the criminals who use or abuse them, then at the hands of a state which stubbornly refuses to acknowledge them, let alone bring their aggressors to justice. Prosecutors and judges quietly bury cases of sexual abuse or exploitation, policemen conveniently sweep the problem under the carpet, and those who are courageous enough to speak out are told to keep quiet, or face being sacked or shunned. Despite the fine words in its constitution, the poor young girls living in this "other" Brazil are absolutely last in anyone's priorities.

As Dean and I recalled everything we had seen and heard over the past year, we agreed that this – the injustice – was the greatest evil stalking this vast motorway. We had travelled 1,500 miles and yet not once had we found a case where a girl's abuser, pimp, brothel owner, trafficker, or even murderer, had been tried and jailed. But we *had* heard of so many cases which had been dropped or left dragging on for years, or had not even been investigated at all. In the "other" Brazil, mothers could push their ten-year-olds into prostitution, fathers could abuse their daughters, pimps could transport and trade young girls like merchandise, and truck drivers could do whatever they wanted, all without fear of punishment or retribution. No wonder their victims ended up believing they were worth nothing – at least no more than the 30 or so reals they were sold for.

The beauty of Fortaleza didn't even come close to that of those young faces of injustice whose lives had marked ours: twelve-year-old Jéssica, drugged, trafficked, and sold – and still seeing the woman who did it walking past her every day in the street; Cássia, thirteen, corrupted by her mother, abused by her uncle, then sold by her cousins – none of whom had paid for their crimes; Mara, sixteen, sitting on that wall in Salgueiro, trapped in a world of drug abuse and sex slavery, and all because of a landlord who still lives above her. Little Sabrina, ten, from Lagoa Grande, still being sold by the hour to a man who knows he can get away with it; and the grieving mothers of tragic fourteen-year-old Natiele and twelve-year-old Ana Flávia, crushed not just by their loss but by the fact their daughters' killers are still driving up and down that motorway, unpunished and unrepentant.

Then there was Leilah, or Leidiane, the very first girl we had met, standing on that lonely patch of earth back in Governador Valadares, and today lost in a tragic cycle of abuse and addiction. Our greatest regret was not being able to offer her a way out. That poor young girl did, though, inspire this journey and a project which we desperately hope will save many girls like her.

As I write this, Meninadança's Pink House in Medina is up and running, and is already making a real difference in the lives of more than sixty young girls, many of whom are blighted by child prostitution. Teenagers who had previously shown no interest in finding help, or were too hurt to believe it, cautiously signed up, and are now coming along every day, finding safety, love, friendship, and people they can trust. The hope that had once been mere dying embers inside them is now beginning to burn brighter and stronger.

Many of those girls started the dance classes timid and ashamed to look at themselves in the mirror, but are now reveling in that reflection, discovering their own beauty and self-worth. We have even taken the girls to perform in nearby towns, where they danced in packed town squares and brought a message to other girls there to stand up against abuse and to not suffer in silence.

Our "Changing Minds" programme is also beginning to challenge the way abuse and exploitation is seen in Medina and the surrounding region, going into schools, churches, workplaces, and communities with a message we hope will change the reality of girls' lives for generations to come. We recently unveiled a huge piece of street art, a mural painted by the Pink House girls on a town centre wall, calling people to look differently at the girls in their town and entitled "Open Your Eyes: Your Look Can Transform Our Lives".

Meanwhile, girls who were once bitter rivals because of Medina's violent turf wars have become close friends. This has been one of the most amazing things we have witnessed. Before we opened the Pink House, people told us never to mix girls from those two areas of town that are at war, warning that it would end in aggression or even bloodshed. Even when we started the dance classes locals told us not to put girls from these two parts in the same group. But the dance, the shared experience, and the irresistible sense of hope have broken down these barriers. We are now seeing those girls dancing together, laughing together, comforting each other, and even praying for one another. It is having a knock-on effect on their parents and friends, and incredibly we are seeing the possibility of an end to the turf wars which have ripped apart these communities for decades.

Our vision is to replicate what we have started in Medina in other towns along the BR-116, and we are already planning a second project, possibly in the town of Cândido Sales, the next town north of Medina. We also hope to support and equip others trying to intervene in other communities, providing them with materials, training, ideas, and other practical help. And our Project 116 is already starting to tell the motorway's untold stories, bringing international attention to individual cases which authorities thought could be buried and forgotten without anyone hearing or caring. Fábio, that brave children's councillor we got to know in Cândido Sales, is working with us, uncovering cases that have been deliberately hushed up or filed away in many other towns and communities along the BR-116.

Mariana, meanwhile, the first girl we managed to rescue, has never looked back. She is another reason why we have hope. Everyone warned she was beyond saving, yet all she needed was a simple lifeline, a chance to put the past behind her and start again. When Mariana recently turned sixteen, we threw a big birthday party – to make up for the other fifteen which no one celebrated. I wept as I saw her, beaming, radiant, surrounded by new friends and family. I could hardly believe she was the same girl we had found, less than a year ago, dancing lifelessly inside that dark, oppressive roadside brothel.

"I never thought I'd ever be happy," she told me. "But I think God saw me. He told you to come and get me, and now he's taken all my pain and sadness away. I'm so grateful."

\*\*\*

Before leaving Fortaleza, Dean and I discovered an interesting fact – that the BR-116 doesn't actually end in the city, it starts there. Just a few streets back from the beachfront was mile zero, not mile 2,819, as we had thought. And for us, too, being there felt more like the beginning of our journey than the end, one which seemed so much more important than the one we'd just finished, one which may take a lifetime and perhaps longer to complete. We don't know everything that will happen along its route, but we are determined to follow it to the end, to press forward, and never give up, until the day girls are protected and valued, until child prostitution is no longer tolerated, until God's light and love penetrate every dark place, even in the remotest corners of Brazil. We invite you to join us.

# meninadança

hope. healing. justice.

For more information about Meninadança´s work rescuing girls from child prostitution on Brazil´s BR-116 motorway please:

Email: office@meninadanca.org

Go to: www.meninadanca.org

Follow:
facebook.com/meninadanca
twitter.com/meninadanca

Write to:
Meninadança
PO Box 11116
Stansted
CM24 8LL
UK

You can contact Matt Roper at:
matt.roper@meninadanca.org
twitter.com/mattroperbr